WHEN GOD SPEAKS

Maresa DePuy
with
Elijah Sebuchu

Contents

About Uganda	4
Forward	7
Introduction	14
1. I was Born in a Swamp	18
2. Relationship is Better than Meat	38
3. In the Blink of a Eye	59
4. Through the Dust	83
5. 10 + 7 + 188	107
6. Oasis of Joy in a Desert of Dispair	134
7. To Lead is to Serve	156
8. Empowering the Next Generation	174
9. Got Faith?	197
Meet Pastor Elijah	217
History of Hands of Love Foundation	220

About Uganda

Uganda is a country in East Africa roughly the size of the state of Oregon, teeming with 45 million people, nearly 10 times that of Oregon. This densely populated country is the **youngest in the world**, with more than half of its inhabitants below the age of 15. An estimated 3.2 million of these children are orphans.

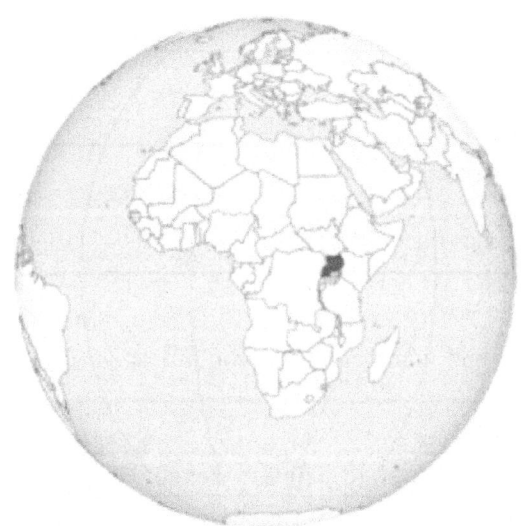

Uganda became independent from British rule in 1962. Tribal warfare ensued. The Ugandan people were brutalized under the dictatorial regimes of Milton Obote and Idi Amin. Finally, in 1986, with the election of Yoweri Museveni as President of Uganda, the country entered a period of relative stability and peace.

Just as Uganda was moving toward political stability, the HIV/AIDS epidemic struck. This country was one of the hardest hit and lost almost an entire generation of adults in a few years. The cultural practice of polygamy and the widespread abuse of women contributed to the rapid spread of the disease.

Years of war, genocide, and disease dealt Uganda severe disadvantages in standards of living, health, education, and prosperity. Most Ugandans continue to suffer from extreme poverty.

- Roughly **40% live on less than $1.25** per day.
- Only **8% have access to electricity** and even less than that have **running water**.
- Most live in **mud and wattle huts**.
- The majority work at subsistence farming, making barely enough to feed their own families.
- **Child labor is common** and many children drop out of school to work or to marry.
- **57% of children do NOT complete primary school**. Less than 30% even enroll in secondary school (begins in grade eight) and only **2% graduate**.
- Most girls marry by the age of 18 and immediately bear children. Less than half of their births will be attended by skilled medical care, so many will die in childbirth. There are only **eight doctors per 100,000 people** and most are inaccessible to the average Ugandan.
- Uganda also suffers from persistent belief patterns that tolerate child sacrifice, cannibalism, polygamy, female genital mutilation,

tribalism, domestic abuse, and the subjugation of women in general.

There are **not enough government resources** to feed, house, clothe, and educate Uganda's orphans. The **children are left to fend for themselves**. The lucky ones have old grannies or sympathetic neighbors who may help. These older relatives and friends are barely able to care for themselves and their own, so their efforts are inadequate to meet the child's needs. Children without support systems end up on the streets, begging for food, eating out of trash bins, drinking out of stagnant pools, running from dangers, wandering alone – hungry and scared. Almost all forgo education. It is a hopeless plight for most and breeds a cycle of generational poverty.

Forward

Last Year, I stepped out of my First World comfort and into Third World reality as I humbly accepted the role of Executive Director for Hands of Love and shortly thereafter made my first visit to Hands of Love in Uganda. It was an amazing and eye-opening experience filled with a kaleidoscope of emotions. As soon as I stepped outside the doors of the airport, I knew I was in a developing country. The dimly lit unpaved parking lot (it was close to midnight), unmarked roadways littered with boda boda's[1] and heavy traffic weaving in and out in all directions, all in a thick haze of dust from the churning of Ugandan clay created a foreboding atmosphere unlike any I have ever experienced. The poverty was apparent and everywhere. Small businesses lined the roadway with street vendors hawking everything from fruits and vegetables to bracelets and home-made brooms with beauty salons, barbershops and motorbike repair shops flying their flags in between. All obscured by the darkness and smoke from grilled street meat adding to the already heavy chalky air. Even at that late hour, there were people on foot everywhere.

Fifty years ago, Uganda, the "Pearl of Africa," was a newly independent republic with a thriving economy, functioning democracy and splendid National Parks. Today, it is a nation that has been devastated by genocide (Idi Amin),

---

[1] East African term for motorbikes – name derived from the transporting of people and good across a border, i.e. border to border, boda boda.

When God Speaks

disease (HIV/AIDS), war (Joseph Kony and the Lord's Resistance Army) and poverty (the results of the aforementioned). Over 80% of the forty-five million people live in abject poverty without running water, electricity and sufficient food. Fifty percent of the population is under the age of 15. It is the youngest country in the world with approximately 3.2 million AIDS orphans. Children are left to raise children. With limited government resources, these children must fend for themselves, often ending up on the streets, begging for food, eating out of trash bins, drinking out of stagnant pools, running from dangers, wandering alone - hungry and scared - breeding a cycle of generational poverty.

It seems overwhelming and hopeless. Yet, there is hope. What I witnessed over the next several days at the Hands of Love Namadhi and Kabaga-Kampala campuses, Maama Eseza's Babies Home, and the Hands of Love Medical Center, showed me what vision, obedience, prayer, faith and unselfishness can do to break that cycle.

Namadhi Campus

The drive to Namadhi was unimaginable. After passing through the city of Jinja and across the Nile river, we headed into the most rural country I have ever seen. The pavement quickly gave way to dirt, and the road we travelled was rough and dusty but busy with trucks, boda bodas, cattle, goats, dogs, and people coming and going from every direction. At some point, the road was reduced to a single rutty, bumpy, muddy lane, almost completely washed out at times. Our vehicle was tossed left and right and up and down as we pressed on to Namadhi. As we continued for about another two- and one-half hours slipping and sliding on this rutty, mud-packed road to seemingly nowhere, I glanced to my right and suddenly all I could see were hundreds of small children in uniform running and jumping and cheering. Pastor Elijah flashed his big smile and said, "Paul, welcome to Hands of Love Namadhi, this greeting is for you." What a beautiful sight! Smiling children lined each side of the road into the campus. They waved branches as they sang. When I stepped out of the vehicle and made my way down the road, they ran to hug me and shake my hand. Words cannot adequately describe the scene or my feelings. I could see the joy in their eyes, the gladness in their hearts, and the happiness all over them.

I spent the day meeting the staff, touring the campus, and learning of its history. This sprawling campus began with one man's vision from God, a piece of inherited land and seven, small mud huts! I was entertained by a group of children who put on a traditional African dance and musical production and then assisted in the herculean task of serving lunch to some 1,300 children. I met with the high school students and prayed over them. The day ended with the handing out of dental supplies and candy to the children before heading back to Kampala, the capital city. It was a full and humbling day.

Kabaga-Kampala Campus

Inasmuch as Kabaga is a suburb of Kampala, the drive to the campus from my hotel was much shorter, but it was just as dusty, muddy and bumpy. And, as you might expect, the traffic was much, much heavier. The roads in and

When God Speaks

around the capital city are clogged with trucks carrying goods from ports in neighboring Kenya, boda bodas carrying 3 and 4 riders at a time and often stacked high with all kinds of cargo, and taxis. The taxis are 14 passenger vans (designed to fit eight) almost always filled to overflowing with people packed in like sardines.

Upon arrival at the Kabaga-Kampala Campus, like Namadhi, the entrance was lined on both sides with children and staff singing and chanting greetings of welcome. Again, it was a moving experience full of joy and happiness. As I made my way down the road, the children followed me giving me high 5's, hand slaps and hugs until we gathered at the center of the campus where the campus director introduced the children to me and told me they had prepared entertainment for my welcome. All the children were gathered in this area and a group of about 10 sang and performed traditional Ugandan dances, welcoming me to Hands of Love. It was awesome and humbling. They all seem so happy. They call me "parent" there, just as the sponsored children call their sponsors "Mom" or "Dad" and truly love being part of a family even if it is 7,500 miles away! The children who do not have sponsors dream of the day they will have a sponsor mom and dad and belong to a family. Family is something many here have never enjoyed apart from Hands of Love. It was great interacting with the children and staff. I couldn't help asking myself, as I looked at those faces and into those beautiful dark eyes, what are their stories and how many more children outside of these walls are living each day just to survive?

When God Speaks

Maama Eseza's Babies Home

As we arrived, we were greeted by Damalie, the supervisor of the Babies home. She informed us it was lunch time and invited us in. As we stepped through the front door, 18 beautiful babies, ages from one to three, were on a large mat on the floor eating lunch. Several of them reached out with food in their hands offering us something to eat. They were all so, so sweet and all look very healthy and are happy. As we sat and watched them eat, Damalie named each one and shared their story. Each was more heart-tugging than the last. One child, 3 days old, was found in a pile of trash along the side of the road. Another, a one year old, was found standing in the pouring rain in the street. Another was abandoned by her mom when her mom left her in the arms of another lady while she went to the restroom but never returned. On and on it went until all 18 were introduced and their stories shared.

The Babies Home has the capacity to house 50 babies. Each house mom will have 5 babies under her care, and each group of 5 will share an apartment of sorts with a separate living room area, crib room, toilet with running water, and an additional room for sick or special needs babies. It is a wonderful set up. Damalie and the house moms are angels on earth and are working miracles with these children. 18 babies are today's capacity due to the lack of resources to support the additional staff needed to care for and nurture more babies.

When God Speaks

Hands of Love Medical Center

The medical center handles women and children only at this time for these groups are the most vulnerable in Uganda. The capacity is 9 patients which is dictated by the number of beds. It is amazing what they do with so little. The lab consisted of a microscope and a few other pieces of equipment for blood work etc. There is a doctor on staff 24/7, and they handle walk-in patients as well as staff and children from Hands of Love. The needs are many for the Medical Center ranging from drugs for healing and pain management to lab equipment. The short-term goal is to expand from 9 beds to 50 by the end of 2021 with the longer-term goal of 100 beds along with identifying and partnering with a local hospital to refer patients with extreme needs.

What a Week

It is difficult to put into words what I experienced during my visit. The only way to truly appreciate and understand what is being done at all the Hands of Love ministries in Uganda is to walk the grounds and interact with the children, staff and teachers. You will experience sensory overload as you see, taste, smell, hear and feel everything around you. Through the obedience, love and compassion of one man, these children who came from nothing, abandoned and left to fend for themselves, have been given the opportunity to be lifted out of the downward spiral of abject poverty. The staff and teachers, who are highly educated, could work most anywhere but choose to be here, ministering to

1,300+ children at each of the campuses with very limited resources, insufficient facilities, meager means, and hard circumstances.

I am confident that God's hands are all over this ministry. Without the vision, unyielding faith and obedience to the Lord by Pastor Elijah Sebuchu and his wife Ruth, Hands of Love would never have been realized. And without the physical, financial and spiritual ongoing support from our donors and sponsors none of what has transpired over the past decade would be possible. God Bless our donors, volunteers, missionaries and all those who sponsor these children. God Bless all the staff and teachers for their sacrifice and devotion to the development of the future leaders of Uganda. And may God continue to bless Uganda, Hands of Love, and the children under their care.

As you read the following pages, you will be encouraged as Maresa unwraps the story of Pastor Elijah Sebuchu, his trials, tribulations, his faith, obedience to God and his calling to save the children of Uganda.

Paul G. Hanson
Executive Director
Hands of Love Foundation

Introduction

The images – forlorn-looking children with bloated bellies - are enough to make North Americans grab their remotes and flip the TV channel. It's but a glimpse of the greater reality of what's happening over there . . . Streets strewn with the bloody carnage of tribal fighting. Emaciated communities stricken by malaria, HIV/AIDS, and tuberculosis.

Some of us engage with the suffering long enough to read an article or a social media post and shake our heads at the ghastly images. But when it comes to taking action, most are intimidated by the immensity of world hunger, poverty, or AIDS. Like surly giants refusing to be conquered, these monstrous epidemics bully us into complacency. Instead of rolling up our sleeves to help, we believe the lie that we are powerless to make a difference.

What if we rejected that lie? What if, instead of changing the channel and scrolling down our social media feeds, what if we *did* something? *Anything.* What if we became the Hands of Love for these children? Suppose we opened our hands to one small act of love reaching to those who have no hope living in a world of poverty and injustice. What if this one act of love created by our outstretched hand grew into a few hands and, before we knew it, our hands birthed an outpouring of change that forever altered lives for the better?

When God Speaks

Imagine if every child left on the streets or in the bush to fend for themselves had hope, peace and protection from disease, crime and violence. Imagine if every child wandering from nowhere to nowhere had a home, parents, food and water. Imagine if every child caught in the downward spiral of abject poverty had opportunity and a way out. Imagine if ALL of Uganda's 3.2 million orphans were empowered to reach their full potential through, love, care, food, shelter, security and education giving them a hope for the future.

Doing small things with great love has a lasting impact. Pastor Elijah Sebuchu is the Hand of Love whose small acts of kindness have extended into the lives of thousands of African orphans. The fact that you are reading this book very likely means that you too can become a Hand of Love.

As a young girl, I also developed a sense of right and wrong, though my surroundings differed drastically from Elijah's. At age ten, I sat in the back seat between my two brothers begrudgingly straddling the "hump" of our 1978, wood-paneled Plymouth station wagon. To deter pinching wars between my brothers and me, our mother's reading sessions magically condensed the nineteen-hour road trip from New Jersey to Central Illinois. Our brains sponged every word mom read from *To Kill a Mockingbird*.

In lieu of DVD players, smart phones, and tablets, we tuned our ears to Harper Lee's enthralling story of Scout and her brother Jem's small-town Alabama adventures during the years of racial segregation. Lee's potent story made a lasting impression. The grit of her characters—the heroic honor of some, and the blood boiling hatred of others—made me want to live better.

Strong convictions or not, I was pretty much oblivious to my African brothers and sisters on the other side of the globe who were dying from AIDS and running from kidnappers who wanted to sacrifice their organs. I was too busy watching the Brady Bunch, roller blading with friends, and annoying my brothers to "extending my hand" to others less fortunate.

Thirty years later, my husband, two children, and I were vacationing at the Georgia lake home of dear friends who support a network of orphanages in Uganda, East Africa. As we spent Labor Day weekend relaxing together, we heard about Hands of Love, an organization that educates and empowers more than 2,600 abandoned and orphaned children. The more we listened, the more invested we became. Question by question, we peeled back layers of the founder's story.

During our drive home to Charleston, we found ourselves unable to think or speak of much else. We were hooked. We weren't questioning *if* we should do something to help these children in Uganda, but rather, *what* we should do? We scratched our heads wondering where to extend our hands. And if it would make a difference.

Our family prayed on it and made the decision to sponsor a five-year-old Hands of Love boy named Samuel. But, still, one phrase continued to plague me each night as I crawled into my king-sized, memory-foam bed.

On average, the staff at Hands of Love turns away eighty children a day.

Had I misunderstood my friend's words? "*Eight* children?" Nope. My hearing was crystal clear. "At both orphanages combined, there are about *eighty* kids turned away each day due to lack of resources," my friend had said.

One year later, with "the eighty" in mind, my husband and I purchased two plane tickets to Uganda. This book is the story of an organization—the story of one life. It's for the "turned away" that we journeyed far to Hands of Love, to meet the blessed ones who live in an oasis of hope amidst a desert of death and disease. And, it's *for* the eighty that we decided to interview the man—the one who simply asked, "What can *I* do?"

Elijah Sebuchu extended his hands into the vast fold of Uganda's poverty. Thousands of life-saving touches began. He was just one person—only a small boy. But he believed he could change lives.

Beautiful things happen when grace pairs a willing man with a God who is searching for someone to serve the abandoned and hungry. Beautiful things emerge from the stretching out of one hand to another to form a pair of hands reaching into the folds of abject poverty.

Hands that can transform lives.

But it all begins with a single act of love and obedience.

1

I Was Born in a Swamp

Two swollen, muddy feet provided her only means of transportation from the midwife's home. Nausea and fatigue bullied her as she counted each step to monitor her labor . . . *58, 59, 60*. She had walked seventeen of her twenty-seven-mile journey. The pain swelled—paralyzed. A single drop of sweat snaked down her back. She inhaled and kept moving. At twenty-two steps between contractions, a harsh realization came: she would not make it home. Nineteen-year-old Eseza would give birth in a sweltering, mosquito-infested Ugandan swamp. Staggering, spent, and afraid, she crumpled into the tall, wet grasses with an agonizing moan. No one, other than the flies, paid attention.

A fly zigzagged the reeds and lit on Eseza's leg. She channeled all her strength for one last push. Covered in a milky mixture of vernix and amniotic fluid, Elijah Sebuchu took his first breath. With a faint cry, his reflexes bounced his tiny arm against the leg of his barely conscious mother. God had delivered a scrawny baby who would grow into a lanky, bony boy, who would grow into a giant of a man, who would leave his indelible mark on the country of Uganda forever.

From his first cry, Eseza struggled to provide. There was no clean water, no bed, not even a towel to bundle him. She tore off the bottom of her filthy *ekikkubiro*[2] dress and swaddled the baby. No nurse or husband were there to hold the child while she recovered. A hot tear etched her cheek. "Help me, God. We need you now." She clutched the squirming baby, gingerly stood, and stared down the endless road home.

Home was a mud and wattle hut in Bugatto Village, Uganda, East Africa where Eseza lived with her husband, three—now four—children, and other wives. The difficult pregnancy had passed, but her relief soon faded. There was another mouth to feed with an already scarce food supply. She couldn't rely on her absentee husband, who came and went as he pleased, had eleven other wives, and countless children that were every bit as hungry as her own.

But one thought kept resurfacing. The moment she first caught her newborn baby's gaze, Eseza sensed the extraordinary. Something shifted. An irresistible force overcame her. She tasted the sweetness of it, and it made her hungry for more.

It was hope.

*****

"I knew God had given me an extraordinary gift; the day Elijah was born. Before he could speak, I believed he was set apart for something significant." Forty-three years later, a quiet awe hushes the room as Eseza Nagguka tells two Americans about her son's humble beginnings. My husband and I have been graciously welcomed into the living room of her cinder block home, located a

---

[2] A garment, typically worn by poor women, made from a traditional Ugandan gown and used bed sheet.

When God Speaks

few miles from the swampy birthplace. We began our journey to Uganda at Charleston International Airport in our home state of South Carolina. We boarded three planes, a subway, a van, and two cars to interview our friend, Pastor Elijah Sebuchu, and to visit his mother's remote village outside Kampala City.

The weighty story presses down on us. Remembering to breathe, I exhale. *She was one of twelve wives who shared a husband, barely potable water, and little food. She walked mile after mile barefoot and pregnant. It's a miracle she didn't die.* And it's a miracle the baby survived; the first of many miracles God would perform to protect his life again and again.

On the wall above Eseza, Jesus is rendered in acrylics, framed in plastic, and hung on a single nail. His blue eyes keep watch over our interview. Beneath the framed Savior, six-foot-four Elijah Sebuchu sits next to his mother. I've never met Mother Teresa. I wonder if meeting her might feel a bit like today. I'm moved by this five-foot-three African mother. Graced by her peaceful countenance, I am awed by the power stirring beneath her quiet, gentle surface.

Her son's strong presence floods the room with warmth; a toothy, magnetic smile highlights his boyish face. His already charming bass voice is rendered more appealing by an African accent. His mother's strong, yet feminine, hands punctuate weighty words that paint a picture of their struggles. I fear the depth and color of her story, delivered in her percussive Lugandan tongue, might be lost in her son's translation. But as Elijah continues, the opposite happens. Their symbiotic mother-son bond fleshes out far richer tones and details. We are drawn into their story.

When God Speaks

"My baby was falling very sick every day with various illnesses, including malaria and diarrhea. I had nothing—nobody was giving me any help." Worry knits lines across Eseza's round, freckled face. She locks eyes with Elijah, who smiles his reassurance. "I didn't know if he would survive. He fell sick almost every day."

Eseza's deep-brown eyes telegraph resilience and joy. Her stubbornness refused despair. "But I knew in my heart that God was going to keep us safe."

What's in a Name

When an American couple is expecting today, many do what is second nature when researching a question: "Google it." They simply type "boy baby names" into the little white box under the famous seven rainbow-colored letters. But on the other side of the globe in Eseza's village, naming babies takes a different approach. If we time traveled back to 1969 and sat with Eseza in the Kasimba clan among the Baganda tribe, choosing a baby's name wouldn't require a Google search. But we would need some hens and a thatched roof hut. They're a dime a dozen in Uganda.

*****

A few days after his swamp delivery, Eseza's son slept tucked in the crook of her strong arms. The pair sat shaded by the roof overhang outside a mud hut. Five chickens were brought before them. The baby's grandfather and chief of the Kasimba clan, George William Bakulumpaji, had selected a name for each

When God Speaks

hen. The infant stirred, perhaps sensing his mother's angst as she awaited the ancestors' choice.

In the Kasimba clan, a child's name was determined by throwing hens atop the roof of the chief's hut. The first hen to fall determined the child's name. Eseza stared at the poultry with a humbling realization that five chickens were about to make or break her son's identity.

The hens were simultaneously thrown on the roof. In a flurry of feathers, the animals bounced, rolled, and dropped. One hit the red clay several seconds before the other four. A terracotta dust cloud appeared. The hen lay motionless in a stunned stupor, then rose, shaking off the fall. The onlookers erupted into joyful shouts. Eseza beamed as she remembered the name given to the hen that fell first: "Ssebukyu."

The ancestors had spoken through chickens. They'd chosen her son, Ssebukyu (which means warrior), to be a leader. For thousands of years, warrior heroes named Ssebukyu have led the Kasimba clan. Eseza now had a tremendous responsibility: to train up a warrior. A leader who will stand against the enemies of his people. What she didn't know was, the people for whom baby Elijah will one day stand, belong not only to the Kasimba clan—or even to Uganda—but to Jesus Christ, the Savior of the world.

Though Ssebukyu will be the name used by his family and clan members, he will later receive his Christian name, Elijah. (In 1984, a school registration spelling error altered his family name from Ssebukyu to the Sebuchu spelling used today.)

Elijah's appointed time and name were established. He was to be a Ssebukyu: a warrior leader who will wage war against Uganda's fierce adversary: poverty. But before baby Elijah could begin such warfare, there was other work to do. For warriors don't become warriors overnight. Little did he know, he was about to enter God's training ground of suffering.

Warrior Training

As Ssebukyu grew, his struggle to survive mounted. Dangers that boggle western brains barraged his frail life: wound-infesting insects; snakes, lions and other wild beasts; measles, tetanus, filthy water, and disease-ridden mosquitoes. Health care was not an option. And there was hunger. *Always* hunger. The fragile lives of Elijah and his family hung in the balance of poverty-induced conditions.

"After the naming ceremony, my husband disappeared," Eseza says. "He returned one day with a new wife, but no suitable hut was available. He forced us to leave and take up residence in the pit latrine." The rancid air and germ-infested surroundings were barely fit for the chickens who lived there during the rainy season. Degraded and humiliated, Eseza had no choice but to consider the latrine their new home.

"At night, my mother would take some wood into the pit latrine. Inside, there was a hole in the dirt floor where others had defecated. She would use the wood to cover the hole so we could sleep there. The smell was awful, but at least we had a roof and shelter from the rain."

When God Speaks

Many poor Ugandan mothers in desperate situations give up. Unable to provide proper food and shelter, their homeless children roam the streets, picking trash and fending for themselves. "If my mother could survive such conditions, no woman has any excuse to abandon their children. Two months later, my grandfather took pity on us and built us a hut. Other than God, I honestly don't know how we survived," Elijah says.

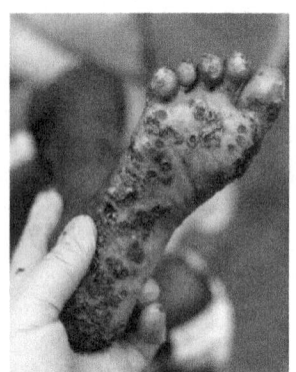

Insects were another fierce enemy in the survival battle. "When he was three years old, my son suffered terribly with jiggers," Eseza remembers. "Jiggers" in Africa are not like chiggers in the U.S., the tiny redbugs that cause a red, itchy, bump for a week. These minute parasites thrive in poor, unhygienic conditions. The bugs burrow into the body, cause terrible pain, and significantly reduce the ability to walk. Infected children bring the parasite to school grounds, exposing others, which leads to widespread infestations and rampant absenteeism.

"I had no access to medicine or even the needles to pluck out my son's jiggers. There was not enough money to buy one needle. Life was very hard. I did not even have salt. I had nothing. My husband was not around."

I think of my own two children. I can't imagine the pain . . . *to have nothing to feed them, no Advil to quiet their fever?* "What did you do?" I hold my breath, waiting for hope.

"I dug, and I dug, and I dug! Then I was able to grow some crops." She smiles. Light erupts in her midnight eyes. With sixty-four years of resolve and wisdom, she explains her simple three-step plan. "I managed to harvest a little food. I would sell a portion to buy a needle to pluck out the jiggers. Eventually, I raised the money to buy medicine to treat Elijah's feet and kill the jiggers."

Elijah recalls the nightmare of the flea-like insects, which burrow into feet, legs, and other body parts, causing them to rot. "Of all the things we suffered, jiggers were the most challenging. Many people, including my mother, can't straighten their legs because of their effects. I often reflect on all our difficulties: the hunger, having no blankets, no clothes . . . But, of all I endured as a child, I think my struggle with jiggers was the worst . . . because they almost killed me.

"I still have scars on my legs and all over my body from jiggers burrowing into my skin. I realize now that if we'd had access to hospitals, the doctors would have amputated my legs. That's how bad my legs were. But we were too poor to afford that."

Thankful for Suffering

I listen to Elijah share his struggles and wonder: Did suffering squeeze out selfishness, or was selfishness a luxury he and his family couldn't afford? Amidst such dire circumstances, they could choose to die or to reach out of their pit of poverty for God. Eseza's choice to trust God in the midst of trials produced a spiritual hunger no earthly food could satisfy.

When God Speaks

"I told my son to be in God at all times. Even if you are in hard situations, when you trust God, He will keep you. I told him God will enable you to overcome anything. The situation may be bad, but God will make a way. In my life, I have seen this work so powerfully."

Heeding his mother's spiritual reminders enabled Elijah to do more than just survive. By walking with God through poverty, illness, starvation, and brushes with death a ripple effect occurs. He thanks God he survived adversity, and thanks Him *for* adversity.

"I believe from the bottom of my heart that the Lord God who created me, saved me, and redeemed me, took me through all this trouble. It was preparation for the ministry. My ministry is to reach out to the suffering, the poverty-stricken, people struggling with sin, with complacency, with hopelessness and death—children with nothing. It's why I exist. I don't regret these trials. No! Instead I thank God for all those experiences."

Poverty, Polygamy, and Pit Latrines

As the fourth of thirty-eight children in a polygamous family, Elijah's home life was crowded and food was scarce. "When I was growing up, people believed more wives equals more success. Today, people are divided. Thirty to forty percent of our population thinks it's wrong to marry more than one wife. Others say it is a private affair. If the person has means, let him do what he wants. Not when I was growing up. Polygamy was widely acceptable."

Out of three hundred huts in Bugatto Village, only three had monogamous families. The men with one wife were regarded as outcasts. "It was considered stupidity of the highest order for a man not to have multiple wives. Having multiple wives was a source of pride—it increased your income. There was lots of land and much work to be done. If you had fifteen wives, at five a.m. you could command them: 'All of you, go out in the field and dig. Now!'"

But more wives meant more children. In Elijah's household, starving kids were plentiful and empty bellies were the norm. "There was some food but, given the polygamy, there were over one hundred people in my dad's huts." What little food they had, they shared. "I was nineteen years old before I ate a meal that filled my belly."

Inside their hut, "there was a lack of space. We had no toilets or washrooms. There was one pit latrine. No kitchen. I never had a blanket." Clothing was scarce and shoes rare, especially for women and children. "I received my first pair of shoes when I was fifteen. I walked *many* miles barefoot to and from school until the dress code required shoes."

The Value of Hard Work

Elijah and I have both walked fifty-one years on this earth and yet I am struck by the weight of what he has lived. And what I have not. I am stung by the ease and innocence missing from his childhood years while I played with my doll house, Slinky, and Weebles that wobble but don't fall down.

When God Speaks

The doll-house builder—my grandpa—used to push me on a burlap sack swing until I was dizzy. Elijah's grandfather took him out into the bush to dig beginning at age four.

"He woke me up early to go dig, not because he needed the hole but because he wanted me to be a hard worker. My grandfather used a hole to teach me to be a hardworking man."

His grandfather was drawn to little warrior Elijah and his mother, whose patient disposition and depth of character gained the chief's favor. Such attention brought privileges, as well as tall expectations.

"I am not training you to be a digger." His grandfather's advice carried weight for young Elijah. "I don't want you to grow up and be a farmer. When the ancestors named you, they chose Ssebukyu. You are going to be a great leader and great leaders don't farm. But I'm training you to be responsible, to wake up, and work hard. Leaders have to be responsible."

Another family encounter fueled Elijah's work ethic—an experience much more disturbing than digging holes.

*****

Young Elijah hurried down the road from his school to Bugatto Village. He was nearly home. "Kampala is the capital city of Uganda," he recited, as he speed-walked the rocky road. "The Buganda tribe is the largest tribe in Uganda . . ." This morning's social study lessons ran through his bright, young mind. *Mommy will smile when she hears what I learned today, if she is not too tired.*

When God Speaks

Elijah's pregnant mother had been moving slower than usual. He didn't know why, but the night before, he overhead her begging his father for something. She'd been crying, a sound that always tugged at his tender heart.

He looked up and recognized the clearing in the trees. Home was just ahead. He turned into the clearing and skipped over to their hut. A few steps from their home, Elijah was met with the distressing sound of his mother's cries. He crouched beneath the crude hole in the mud wall "window" to listen.

"I am sick," Eseza moaned. "If only you could find a small bit of cow liver to give me strength. My work is suffering . . . I can cook more and dig for more crops if you give me the liver. I am so weak . . . please."

It hurt Elijah to hear Eseza beg for food. He rose slowly and peeked through the window into the hut. His mother pulled herself along the dirt floor toward her husband. Her pregnant belly and swollen feet, covered in oozing wounds, made it difficult to walk. Her anemia made it almost impossible to manage the daily workload Elijah's father demanded she complete.

Elijah won't easily forget the disturbing moments that came next.

He watched in horror as his father grabbed his pregnant mother and beat her until she stopped crying. "No! You stupid, foolish woman! Where would I get a cow's liver? Even if I could get liver, do you think I would give it to you?! You must be out of your mind. This will teach you to ask me again."

The series of angry blows left Eseza motionless, lying face down. Her soft sobs broke Elijah's seven-year-old heart. He waited for his father to storm out and then rushed to her side.

When God Speaks

"Mommy! Mommy!" Elijah whisper-shouted. "I am here. It's me, Ssebukyu. Let me fetch you some water. Mommy . . .?" Somehow, Eseza managed the strength to grab her son's hand. She squeezed and Elijah squeezed back. He knew she would survive, but not without his help.

Later that night, Elijah lay on his palm mat trying to sleep. Angry tears flowed as he replayed the disturbing scene over and over. *I have to find a way to buy that cow liver. Tomorrow, after school, I will look for work. I will go dig for my mother, even if it takes me every hour of daylight, every day after school, for weeks. I will get her that liver so she can get stronger.*

"I was only seven years old," Elijah remembers. "But after witnessing that, I promised myself I would work every day so my mother would never suffer again."

My carefree, seventh year of life looked a bit different. While I was eating Jell-O and attending Girl Scout meetings after school in suburban New Jersey, Elijah was digging, hauling produce, washing clothes, and performing odd jobs to earn spare change.

"My mother had no salt or even soap. She would burn swamp grass and use the "salty" ashes to season our food. Instead of soap, we bathed with banana and pawpaw leaves." With every load of bananas, firewood, or charcoal Elijah carried, the family gained a few schillings for a tiny bag of salt[3] or bar of soap.

Many times he was hired for jobs much heavier than his slight, skinny frame could bear. "I could have split up the loads to make them lighter, but my boss would say, 'If you need money, you must carry it all at once! Otherwise I will hire another.' I would consider my sick siblings at home with no water or matches. I had no choice but to take the work." One day while carrying a top-heavy load, ten-year-old Elijah tripped and sustained a painful cracked rib that went untreated until he was an adult. He pressed on in pain feeling that if he paused the work would be given to someone else and the promise he made to himself would be broken.

Darkness Falls

Still driven by his grandfather's lessons, the diligent pastor's workday fades into a work night. Seated beside Elijah in his sturdy SUV, we venture out after dusk. The darkness is thick here, blacker by far than our Charleston nights, where streetlamps and city lights glow. We catch an occasional glimpse of a campfire ablaze beside a mud hut. It pierces the darkness at first, but soon fades beneath the shroud of African nightfall.

---

[3] In Uganda, salt is a precious commodity used to season and preserve food.

When God Speaks

Elijah's face dims. I hear the fear in his voice as he shares childhood memories. "It was beyond dark at night. Pitch black. There was no main source of light, so we had to use paraffin candles."

Whether you are from South Carolina or Uganda, light has a price. In the U.S., we pay our monthly bill to the local electric company. In rural Uganda, one buys fuel for an oil lamp or candle. Elijah counts the cost of light, remembering when he was eleven. Light cost him several weeks of after-school labor weaving two grass baskets. And it almost cost him an arm.

"My mother had gone two weeks without any fuel to light a small candle. We had been living in the dark for two weeks! I began making a basket to sell for about five cents. Selling two baskets would buy the fuel to light her candle. But it takes several days to do that type of work. I would go to school and come back at five p.m.

"One afternoon, I came home from school and pulled out my basket. Unaware of the snake inside, I prepared to work, but the snake jumped out and coiled around my neck. I shouted and grabbed its head. My mother heard my shouting and came running." Elijah's warrior instincts prevented a venomous bite, but this wouldn't be his last serpent show down.

Hoping to avoid any creature encounters of my own, I fumble around in a dark hotel room later that night. My hand skims the wall until I reach the switch plate. I flip the switch, not giving it one thought. I trust the light will illuminate the path to my laptop where I check in with family and friends on the other side of the world. I will tell them about my day with Elijah, the basket maker, who lights the way for others. One who lights the way . . .

I consider John the Baptist lighting the way to Jesus. It's exactly what this struggling basket-maker-gone-preacher does:

"There was a man sent from God whose name was John. He came as a witness to testify concerning that light, so that through Him all might believe." (John 1:6-7).

Pastor Elijah testifies to the light. He could have drowned in the ocean of poverty. Instead, as an eight-year-old boy, he stretched out his hand and made a declaration beyond his years: *There has got to be a better life for my mother, my siblings and for the people of Uganda.* Today, he points others to *the* Light at Hands of Love, a network of orphanages and schools that educates and empowers AIDS orphans.

"In Him was life, and that life was the light of all mankind. The light shines in the darkness, and the darkness has not overcome it" (John 1:4-5). The skinny basket weaver transforms swamp reeds to afford a box of matches and a single candle. He strikes the match and sets the wick ablaze. The candle casts a faint glow that pierces Uganda's thick, black shroud.

He may be starving, scrawny, and seemingly insignificant, but he will bring light to the suffering . . . and the darkness will not overcome it.

When God Speaks

Painted Toes and Eyedroppers

I read blogs, Facebook posts, books, and magazine articles about how the North American Church could do more to alleviate suffering. In her book, *Kisses from Katie*, Katie Davis compares serving in a Third World country to "emptying the ocean with an eyedropper. And just when I have about half a cup full of water it rains: more orphaned children from the north migrate to where I live, more abandoned and dead babies are found, more people are infected with HIV."

I must agree with her. Taking my heart to Uganda is like landing in an ocean of poverty with a kayak, an eyedropper, and no paddle. I'm nearly swallowed up by the immensity of the problem. But I don't want to become part of the problem. If all I have is the eyedropper words I type, then one word at a time I will type, emptying the next dropper of the ocean that is drowning Uganda's kids.

How many reading this, including myself, have gone on mission trips and come home hungry to change the world? Did you return ready to forfeit your Starbucks addiction, sell your home, and donate all earthly possessions? But how realistic is that? Would I be helping or hurting? I only know I don't want to live the same way. So, I'm putting it out there: *Lord, on behalf of the North American Church, I ask you to wake us up.*

When God Speaks

In *The Weight of Glory*, C.S. Lewis writes, "You and I have need of the strongest spell that can be found to wake us from the evil enchantment of worldliness." When we suffer, or serve those who do, do worldly things fall away? In Lewis' classic tale, *The Lion, The Witch and the Wardrobe*, the White Witch lures young Edmund into her wicked scheme with a sweet treat called Turkish Delight. Perhaps materialism is the Turkish Delight that numbs our souls and lures us into complacency. Meanwhile, a mother in Africa struggles to buy a single needle to pluck jiggers from her child's feet.

I don't mean to beat anyone up, because I'm right there with you. Instead, I invite you to join this soul-searching journey by asking God, "What hand can I extend and to whom?"

I stood at a rock concert this summer listening to a chock-full stadium of cheering fans. Our feet moved in unison to the pop music's contagious, sunny beat. The light show was mesmerizing. But, all at once, a holy awareness set in. I began to dream about what would happen if the lead singer on stage made an announcement to the crowd. Instead of screaming "Good evening, Charleston. Are you ready to have a good time? Make some noise!" What if instead he were to say, "Good evening, Charleston. Would you like to have a *really* good time? Would you like to experience joy far surpassing the momentary high of a brush with rock stardom? Yes? Open your wallets and search for a dollar. If you have one, hold it up. I'd like you to take that dollar and hand it to the little lady from Hands of Love who will be standing at the front gate. Relish the joy of knowing your dollar will change a child's life in Uganda."

When God Speaks

You may be thinking, "Oh yeah, right. That would never fly at a pop concert." But let's suppose it did. If my calculations are accurate, one thirty-second announcement has the potential to raise enough funds to clothe five-hundred orphans at Hands of Love, maybe more. Who among those smart phone-carrying, beer-buying, social-networking fans could not afford *one dollar*? This is not about guilt. It's about the incredible contrast of lifestyles, the Gospel, and how to reconcile the two.

After spending two weeks in Uganda and returning home, I often have flashbacks. One day, my son and I are sitting in Chick-fil-A, eating a tasty fast-food lunch that costs ten dollars. I scan the line of hungry South Carolinians waiting to order chicken sandwiches and zero in on their feet. South Carolinians, at least the ones where I live, have nice feet. Some are dress-socked and laced in business shoes. Some sport sneakers and others, flip-flops with hot pink pedicures. The vast majority are nice, clean, healthy feet.

My mind flashes to the feet in Uganda. At Hands of Love, we saw few—if any—painted toes among hundreds of shoeless feet. Lots were disfigured, having lost toes to bouts with jiggers. Some injure and lose toes from daily walking miles of rocky, garbage strewn roads. Shoes would help eradicate this problem. It's a simple need and it wouldn't take much to meet it. Why aren't we doing more if Jesus rewards even a single cup of water given in His name?

"And whoever in the name of a disciple gives to one of these little ones even a cup of cold water to drink, truly I say to you, he shall not lose his reward" (Matthew 10:42).

When God Speaks

Writing this book is my cup of water—my extended hand. If I were a lobbyist, I might politick to revamp laws. If I were a multi-millionaire, a grant writer, or a pilot, my contribution would look different. What about you? Do you cut hair, design houses, or run a corporation? There is not a gift our God is unwilling to use for the suffering ones if laid before Him with an open heart.

As for me, I write. I take what I know how to do, and I do it. *And please, Jesus, let it be something. Let it be enough to buy a few kids in Kampala a pair of shoes. And if you'd like me to paint their toes too, I will.*

When God Speaks

2

Relationship Is Better Than Meat

Four-year-old Elijah hacked his hoe into the hard, brick-red soil. Hands this small and young shouldn't be calloused, but his were. Beside him, his mother gripped a homemade shovel speaking words that gripped her children's hearts. She seized any opportunity to speak life to all her children, but especially to her son, who had been marked as a leader in the Kasimba clan.

"Ssebukyu, listen to me," she instructed. "You are going to be a great man and a powerful leader, but you can't lead alone. Leaders must be patient with people. Leaders must be kind and understanding." Young Elijah worked the soil in hopes of producing cassava[4] for hungry bellies. Eseza tilled the soil of his heart. She silently prayed as she dug so that both the garden and her son would bear fruit to feed hungry mouths and souls.

As he grew, it was his mom, not his dad, who consistently parented Elijah, teaching, nurturing, and protecting him. Without his knowledge, Eseza

---

[4] A large thick-skinned tuber that is like the potato when boiled. It is eaten in many tropical countries and used as a source of tapioca.

shadowed Elijah and his siblings on their three-mile walks to primary school, scouting the bush for wild animals and human predators who abducted and sacrificed children. She protected her children from both physical dangers and ignorance by ensuring they reached *Bugonya Primary School* in Uganda's Kayunga district. Though she never progressed past grade four, she constantly stressed the value of education to her children.

*****

"For as long as I can remember, one of the greatest blessings I've had—even up until this day—is my mother." Elijah and I sip coffee together one bright July morning in Kampala. We celebrate the legacy of a mother's wisdom. His memories spotlight *the* person most responsible for molding him into the influential, tour-de-force leader he is today. Eseza Nagguka was more than Elijah's greatest fan. She was a catalyst, driving him towards God's calling.

"As soon as I got the name 'Ssebukyu' my mother knew that I was destined for something. She started speaking into my life that I was going to be a great man. My entire life, I've never heard any negative word from my mother. I have always heard her say, 'You are going to be a great leader.' She has always said: 'Leaders are patient with people. Leaders are kind, understanding, and can't do anything alone.'"

Her words of wisdom sweep over his tongue in a seemingly effortless flow, as if they are written in permanent ink on Elijah's heart. I stare at this international leader who fiercely advocates on behalf of the abandoned and orphaned children of his country—the one who meets with dignitaries and

When God Speaks

speaks at international symposiums. The man who oversees over 300 servant leaders who minister to Uganda's hurting and forsaken. I marvel at the positive influence of one strong, determined mother.

Eseza did not say to her son, "*If* you want to be a great leader someday," but "*When* you are a great leader." She believed, with every fiber of her being, that her son would be an international leader. "Children are apt to live up to what you believe of them," Lady Bird Johnson once said. It's safe to say Elijah lived up to his mother's beliefs.

"She believes so strongly in the importance of education." Elijah's timber, already at bass level, deepens as we discuss one of his greatest passions. "The one thing that drove me was what my mother told me: *A person who is going to be a leader, he must have an education.* She told me this every day: *You have got to build strong relationships with other leaders.*"

"My mother knew that many of these leaders do not speak Luganda," Elijah's native tongue and the language spoken by more than sixteen million Ugandans[5]. "One day, my mother told me of a dream where she watched me gather children from different African tribes. I was addressing them—in which language? English!" To turn his mom's dream into reality and to build international relationships, Elijah pushed himself academically.

Still today, he is pursuing his PhD. in Economic Development at Makerere University where he has received a Master's Degree in Development

---

[5] Luganda is primarily spoken in the southern region of Uganda, including the capital Kampala. http://en.wikipedia.org/wiki/Luganda

and a BA in Project Planning and Management. Upon completing high school, he completed two diplomas of theology from Bishop Tucker Theological College[6] and Mbuya Bible College, in addition to receiving his BA in Christian Ministry from Alpha-Omega Seminary.

Relationship, Relationship, Relationship

Education was a huge household priority, but Elijah's mom placed an even greater emphasis on gaining friendships. Accordingly, it's rare to spend even an hour with this highly educated Ugandan Pastor without hearing him spout his mom's favorite saying:

> *Relationship is better than meat.*

From age four, she consistently fed (and still feeds) the same bread-and-butter proverb to Elijah. "She would not speak this just once a day, but so many times until I would get fed up. *Every day*! As I left for school, she would say: 'Remember Ssebukyu, relationship is better than meat, better than anything you will ever get.' When I was digging: 'Remember son, relationship! When I was laying down to sleep: Never forget to build relationships!' My mother would speak that and sing that until I could feel it as part of my blood. To this day, the most important thing I value—other than God—is relationship. I've seen her live that and I've seen it work! Relationship, relationship, relationship!"

---

[6] Known today as Uganda Christian University.

When God Speaks

Albert Einstein reasoned, "Setting an example is not the main means of influencing another, it is the only means." Eseza influenced Elijah not by her preaching, but by *her living*.

"So many people adored my mother because she valued people and brought them together. She could connect an entire village, even people from different tribes. I thank God for my mother. Even if I were speaking to her now, one of the first four words she would say to me, would be *relationship*."

Eseza and I escape the glaring rays of Uganda's sun one July afternoon. A rare commodity, bottles of clean water, invigorate dry mouths. Freckles dot Eseza's dark, apple-shaped cheeks. No-nonsense, curly, black hair frames her lively eyes. She grins from ear to ear and I see traces of Elijah's smile. I can't decide which is more refreshing: her motherly wisdom or the water. Both quench my thirst for something.

"Who taught you that relationship is better than meat?" I ask.

"I prayed for God to reveal the most important things in life. Because of that prayer, God told me: *Relationship is better than meat*. I tried it myself and realized that it is good to work with people instead of looking for what you can get from them."

In a corner of the world where the scarcity of meat has driven people to eat rats[7], Elijah's mind and empty belly were challenged by God's wisdom. "I

---

[7] *"Living off rats to survive in Zimbabwe"* by Jeff Koinange
http://www.cnn.com/2006/ WORLD/africa/12/19/ koinange.zimbabwe/index.html

told him to work with all people and learn to relate well to people—even your enemies. Your relationship with people will win them from evil to good."

Elijah puts this wisdom into practice more than anything else his mom taught. It is *the* teaching that has won him countless relationships with far-reaching impact for his ministry. "God uses relationships to accomplish what He wants you to do," he says. "This is part of me because I have seen it practically." Because of Eseza's strong relationship with her father-in-law, chief of the Kasimba clan, Elijah was chosen among all the chief's sons and grandsons to inherit the acreage where Elijah would one day build seven mud huts to serve the first group of 188 orphans.

"My mother was a *big* friend of my grandfather, more than all my father's other wives. Why? Because she was the most patient person my grandfather had ever known. Her patience caught his favor. Because of that, I got to spend a lot of time with him, much more than all my siblings. And because of our *relationship*, he appointed me to be his heir."

A Nasty Combination

Living as one of twelve wives tested Eseza's patience. The wicked combination of polygamy and witchcraft wreaked havoc on family dynamics. "My stepmothers bewitched one another. They would harvest my father's feces, dry it, and mix it with the feces belonging to their chosen victim." The bewitched wife was believed to give off a putrid odor when Elijah's father entered her bedroom, causing him to refuse her. "My stepmother's desire to see the other wives die was deeply disturbing to me. It caused bitterness, enmity, and division among our family." As often as possible, Eseza excused herself from the polygamous drama. Her ability to rise above the divisiveness of the other women set her apart in the eyes of her father-in-law.

"My father-in-law loved me. Because of that love, hundreds of children now have a place they call home." Eseza compares her journey with the Bible's Ruth: a poor widow whose humble desire to serve her mother-in-law reaped a life-transforming outpouring from Boaz. Eseza's extended hand—her desire to honor her husband and his father—also brought blessing, a ripple-effect bounty for this generation of Uganda's children and many to come.

"My son took hold of what I taught him. I see this proven by the friends he has from all over the world— including you." Her huge smile blazes trails in a new relationship with friends from a state she's never heard of before this morning . . .

*****

Elijah's car bumps along the dirt drive that approaches his mom's modest house. My stomach does a second combination of back flips at the thought of meeting Eseza. *Maybe a handshake would be ok . . . she is used to meeting wazungu[8] from the West. Or would a hug would be more appropriate? Just how do you greet a superhero?*

---

[8] plural of mzungu, which in East African language means white person or foreigner, particularly those from Europe and other Western countries.

When God Speaks

I notice her right away once we turn into Eseza's driveway. The black and green *gomesi*[9] she wears is quickly upstaged by her dazzling smile. She seems to be jumping. *Jumping?* And what is that strange noise she is making? As we exit the car, what sounds like a high-pitched combination of Indian war cry and cheerleading victory yelp streams from Eseza's mouth as she hops up and down with excitement. She rejoices at the sight of her son and his visitors.

We revel in the joyous reunion and greet her like the supermom she is—one who welcomes big hugs from foreigners.

We haven't yet stepped inside her home and already, she is praying for us. Her strong hands rest on our shoulders. All eyes close. Being with Eseza is a bit like hanging out in a rainforest. You spend enough time around either one and a downpour is likely. Like rain from the skies of a tropical jungle, her mighty prayers cover us, flowing down on our hands.

two women wearing a gomesi.

Her prayers multiply the ripple effect of the tiny extended hand by coming to Uganda.

---

[9] the brightly colored national dress of Ugandan women. Gomesis are fashioned from silk and cotton and typically consist of a top, floor-length skirt and sash. (*The truth about the Gomesi as a National Dress for Uganda Women* by Thomas R Omara-Alwala. http://nilejournal.net/culture/society/gomesi-national-dress-uganda-women)

When God Speaks

Explaining Yourself to God

As a mother raising eleven kids in abject poverty, prayer was a way of life for Eseza. It wasn't optional. Like sleeping and brushing your teeth, it was a required, daily habit.

"At home, my mother would always pray," Elijah says. "We were constantly encouraged to pray. If you went to sleep without prayer, the next day you were not greeted, given food or even water. My mother knew my favorite thing was going to school. If she found I had not prayed, I would not be allowed to go to school. I learned to pray loud enough for her to hear!"

Eseza required regular prayer, but she also taught her children the reason why. "Growing up there was a lot of death. There was famine, flooding, malaria, measles, tetanus, sickle cell disease and war," Elijah explains. "My mom told us: 'The only way to survive this life is by putting your hands in the hand of God, because He will protect you.'

"I used to ask her: 'Mommy, what is prayer?' She would say to me: 'God, who knows the impossible, is able to *do* the impossible. So what you do is explain yourself to this God and He will take care of you.' My mother very clearly told me that it is God who's going to help you."

Eseza explained herself and her trials to the God of the impossible, who enabled her and her children to overcome the odds, including multiple military raids. In the midst of this violence, Elijah's mother taught him another critical lesson about perseverance.

When God Speaks

Curious for more details on the multiple military raids, I ask Elijah about Idi Amin. His eyes dim. He speaks slowly, describing a scene from 1978, when Amin's soldiers ordered the burning of hundreds of huts . . .

*****

Ratt-a-tatt-a-tat-a-tatt. Ratt-a-tatt-a-tat-a-tatt!

"Ssebukyu!" Eseza ordered. "We must go—now!" Nine-year-old Elijah grabbed his favorite stick, the one he always used to stoke the cooking fire and ran after his mom who sped away from their mud hut.

victims of Idi Amin regime recovered by a local farmer

Ratt-a-tatt-a-tat-a-tatt. Ratt-a-tatt-a-tat-a-tatt!

He hated that unmistakable sound. It wasn't very loud yet but he could tell they weren't far off. He ran faster, zigzagging around tree stumps and roots.

His quick, lanky legs carried him quickly, but the rough terrain made it hard to keep up. He raced on trying to catch sight of his mom. Even a glimpse of her had a calming effect.

He never got used to the raids. For years, Idi Amin and his brutes had been scouring Uganda's countryside, pillaging and burning any village they encountered. Bugatto village had fallen prey to military raids so often that Elijah's family assumed a familiar routine when news of the soldiers came. The miserable escape plan included sleeping in the bush for weeks, even months, only to return to a hut that had been wiped clean. The gourds used to collect water: gone. The clay pots Eseza used for cooking: gone. The wooden tree stump "stools" that provided a dry place to sit during the rainy season: gone.

Sleeping in a mud hut was no picnic, but sleeping in the black-as-tar bush was a nightmare. Wild animals emitted eerie howls and screeches. Cougars and lions prowled the makeshift camps, which triggered midnight tree-climbing sessions. Snakes and insects stalked and bit his family. And finding food was a relentless struggle, having fled miles from the village garden.

But starvation and snake bites were the lesser of two evils. Families that remained behind suffered unthinkable violence. Women and their children were raped. The thought of beheadings and other horrific acts committed by Amin's band of beasts kept Elijah's feet moving swiftly as he tried to catch up to his mom.

Some Kind of Crazy

A child should feel secure—protected. He should have a safe, clean bed and loving arms to tuck him in at night. Under a lacy-white canopied bed my own mother tucked me into cotton sheets, not the prickly palm leaves of the bush. Depending on how tired we were, we shared a bedtime prayer.

But for Eseza's family, prayer was mandatory. It was a way of survival. The only way. It was *the* way to call on the God of the impossible to meet them in their impossible situation. Faith that God will lead and protect.

When God Speaks

With no husband in sight and gunfire echoing in the distance, Eseza relied on God alone to protect her family. "Sometimes we would just be sitting at home and suddenly, the soldiers would invade. These men used to rape women—they would even rape small children—in their homes, so we had to run very fast. These men would shoot guns. Even in the bush, they would repeatedly fire off random shots. We had to take cover in the bushes.

"This went on for five years. Frequently, we were forced to sleep with insects, animals, and snakes. When we came back, nothing remained. Not even the cooking pots. But despite all the shooting and looting, I always knew in my heart that God was going to keep us safe."

I exhale and try to put myself into Elijah's size-twelve shoes. I turn from him, trying to hide my tears. Avoiding eye contact, I rummage through my bag for a tissue. Scenes of children watching their mothers being beaten and raped rage through me. Somewhere deep in the recesses of my soul, I could swear I hear a crack. Something has broken. It hurts to breathe. But I cannot change the channel because the ones who suffered through this living hell are sitting here in front of me—they are no longer just figures appearing on my TV screen.

"Weren't you scared?"

"I was afraid, but my mother was there."

"But what about your dad? Your dad is the one who is supposed to protect you." My western, monogamous upbringing is at odds with his polygamous one.

When God Speaks

"As the father of thirty-eight children, there was no way for my dad to protect me." Elijah's matter-of-fact tone is unsettling. "He was a busy man. For me, when I was growing up, I knew the responsibility for managing the home was on the woman. Sometimes months would go by without seeing my dad because he was very busy working and there were 100 people in our household. From this, I learned that men were supposed to give orders and produce children."

My eyes widen in disbelief. The more I learn about what supermom Eseza was up against, the mightier she seems. *Men give orders and produce children?* I am jarred—and frankly a bit angered—by this culture of wives by the dozen, who-knows-how-many concubines, and too-many-to-count children where men bark orders and women dig. I wrestle to grasp a neighborhood where husbands disappear when soldiers appear. This is some kind of crazy, the kind I'm certain I wouldn't survive.

Don't Run Away, Stay

Though running to escape brutal soldiers was a means for survival, Eseza and her family always returned to their village when it was safe. In fact, Elijah was taught to resist the urge to disappear when times got hard, like so many men had done. "During the 1980 famine, when our village was struggling, my father disappeared." Elijah says. "But every Saturday, my mother took me to the bush to till the garden with my sister, Esther Ruth Nakabazzi. She taught me that whenever there is calamity, you don't run away. You work very hard to overcome it. Through the years I've had *many*—not one—*many* opportunities to leave Uganda. But I remember what my mother taught me when I was ten years old: *when there is trouble, you stay.*

"I don't believe in running away from problems. I believe in facing them, challenging them, and changing them. I encourage people in Uganda: if there are problems in your marriage, you stay. Problems with your kids? You stick with them. You face the problems and challenge them—change them! Even Uganda's trouble with AIDS, I have always believed that there is a solution somewhere. When people see so many children everywhere, many say, 'The need is too big.' But even with this big need, every one of us can do something and eventually—eventually—the work will be done."

Digging In

Eseza was hard pressed to find a solution for survival during Uganda's 1980 famine. Times were especially difficult and the temptation to give up loomed large.

"During the famine, my husband ran away for eight months. I was left there to die with Esther, Elijah and my other children. We had no food . . . nothing." The memory of desperate times darkens her, but only momentarily. Because she is a mother who is not given over to giving in. She doesn't run the other way when trouble comes. Instead, she digs in and . . . she digs!

When God Speaks

Blessed are the Givers

Elijah understands the pain that Uganda's hungry children experience. The '80-'81 famine left his and many other families desperate for food. But resourceful Eseza had a plan. When things were just beginning to look hopeless she put all her children to work in their garden planting cassava, beans, corn, *matooke*[10] and sweet potatoes. Surviving on "tea" made from grass and whatever they could forage in the jungles, they prayed and waited for the crops to bear anything edible.

matooke

"When the food was finally ready," Eseza says, "I felt it was important to teach the children giving and also forgiveness. So we gave food to others, including Elijah's father. It was a big opportunity to teach them lessons: *to forgive and to give away*."

At the time, Elijah and his starving siblings weren't happy with Eseza's lesson in giving. But today it bears fruit as he ministers to vulnerable children, the sick, and the poor. "I began to see that when you work very hard you not only change the situation for others but eventually even *your* situation will change. That is exactly what happened. We worked very hard planting crops. Once the rains came, it took about one hundred days before the crops were ready

---

[10] A plantain-like, green banana grown abundantly throughout Uganda. Matooke is a staple food for most Ugandans.

to harvest. Eventually, there was a lot of food. Mom refused to let us begin eating before we did two things: first, we would take a portion to our church. Next, my mother would send me and my sister with baskets of food to different homes among the village."

Elijah remembers learning the important lesson of reaping what you sow[11]. "We knew that if we gave away this food, things will get better for other people first. We also believed that when you give, God blesses you, and then eventually things will be better for you. That lesson has stuck with me! Even when I see people leaving Uganda for greener pastures, this sticks with me."

My stomach growls, a reminder that lunch time has come and gone. *Were they cheerful givers—Elijah and his family—walking from hut to hut giving away their harvest? It's easy to give to others when your belly is full, but when you, yourself, are starving...?* I'm amazed by how a poor family, with no access to the Living Word, refreshed others by living out the Word.

"One person gives freely, yet gains even more;

another withholds unduly, but comes to poverty.

A generous person will prosper;

whoever refreshes others will be refreshed"

Proverbs 11:24-26.

---

[11] Galatians 6:7-8

When God Speaks

A Mother's Words: God's Life Preserver

Eseza engrained words of purpose and identity into Elijah —*You are a leader. You are chosen. You are special.* Her powerful words became a supernatural life preserver for her son. "She treated me in a special way. I held the truth close to me, especially when I was a teenager, that there was something special within me. I would remember my mother's words at night when I walked in the bush and when I made difficult decisions. I would always remember that there was something special within me." When others were getting mixed up in violence, drinking, promiscuity, or stealing, Eseza's life-giving prayers and promises guided Elijah toward wiser ways—ways that kept him from danger and pointed him toward his calling.

"In Uganda, we have lost so many. Maybe two percent of my generation has survived, but many people I grew up with—*many* of them—have been exterminated by HIV/AIDS. The words I grew up hearing my mother speak, I think God used them to preserve me. Because I knew that if I died, I would not rise up to be the leader my mother always talked about."

The ripple effect of Eseza's words continues today. Her life-preserving prayers buoyed her son and birthed a wave of change for their poor, polygamous culture and a tsunami of blessing for the children of Uganda. "My mother would lay hands on me, pray silently, and speak over me that I would be a great leader."

Other world and national leaders have also had the guidance of a Mother's prayer. If Nancy Lincoln and Eseza sat down for tea, they would have plenty in common. Nancy's son, Abraham, was powered by his mother's prayers, which spilled over into the transformation of an entire nation.

"I remember my mother's prayers," Lincoln once said, "and they have always followed me. They have clung to me all my life."

When God Speaks

When God Speaks

A Sweet Gift

Speaking truth and praying "prayers that cling" impacts children who are willing to receive. I picture Eseza with Elijah and don't envision the rolling eyes of a teenager who rejects his mother's praise. I yearn for my words and prayers to immerse into my two wonderful, westernized teenagers so they too will become those who outstretch their hands to others. Prayers and truth are bricks in a child's foundation. But bricks topple without mortar. It's the mortar—the missing ingredient—that defines the most essential parenting lesson: *above all, love your children.*

When Elijah was emerging as a leader in middle school, Eseza recognized greatness. "He loved the children—especially the children," says Eseza. "He was hard working and he did not anger easily. I observed the qualities of a great leader: Elijah loved people. He was forgiving, giving and respectful to the parents. He was humble. Special intelligence and wisdom were upon him. I always prayed to God and spoke into his life that he was going to be a national leader who would touch many lives."

But the glue that bonded all her efforts to shape Elijah into a man of integrity was love. "I also loved him and spoke that love into his life. If you want a person to receive what you are speaking to him, you need to love that person. And I loved him most."

Love trumps all.

When God Speaks

"If I speak with human eloquence and angelic ecstasy but don't love, I'm nothing but the creaking of a rusty gate. If I speak God's Word with power, revealing all His mysteries and making everything plain as day, and if I have faith that says to a mountain, 'Jump,' and it jumps, but I don't love, I'm nothing. If I give everything I own to the poor and even go to the stake to be burned as a martyr, but I don't love, I've gotten nowhere. So, no matter what I say, what I believe, and what I do, I'm bankrupt without love" 1 Corinthians 13:1-3[12].

"Love them most." It's my final lesson in raising children who will put love into action. I review scenes from my life as a mother. *If I pray eloquent, powerful prayers for my children and speak all kinds of truth I learned at Bible Study, but nag and guilt them, and stare at my iPhone more than I look into their eyes, then my words are fingernails on the chalk board of their hearts. None of us gains anything. We are all bankrupt.* It's all held together with love. Not love the thought, but love the verb.

I watch Eseza walk out the back door of her cinder block home with a machete in her hand. She swings it, rhythmically hacking off sugarcane stalks that will become our gift. It's as if she could harvest the sweet stalks blindfolded. Within minutes, she hands us our love offering.

The bamboo-like stems lay heavy across our laps as we drive away. We're surprised to learn that sugarcane has tremendous nutritional benefits. It

---

[12] *The Message* translation

boosts immunity, lowers cholesterol, wards off kidney stones, and prevents fatigue.

    The gifts she gave bring nourishment: health for our bodies and wisdom that feeds our souls. I feel full. Satisfied. Rubbing shoulders with Elijah's mom has graced me. I'm invigorated and challenged to speak life over, pray for, and above all, love my children more than ever.

3

In the Blink of an Eye:
the Making of a Leader

Our Charleston home overflows with neighbors, friends, and family. Appetizers have been warmed, candles lit, and ice bucket filled. Everything's in place. Everything except the guests of honor. Elijah and his wife Ruth are in our guest room with the door closed. As people of prayer, their debut at tonight's home-grown Hands of Love reception has likely brought them to their knees to talk with God. Because that is how they roll.

I knock at the door. "Hello?"

"Yes, please come in," Elijah says. "Are you ready for us?"

"Yes. We are ready. Please come meet our friends."

There are certain people who simply walk into a room and the atmosphere changes. Elijah Sebuchu is such a person. Leadership is in his blood—his commanding presence beckons those around him. People are drawn to him. He enters our kitchen and voices drop low. He begins to shake hands, looking each *mzungu*[13] in the eye to offer a sincere greeting and warm smile.

---

[13] The East African word, *mzungu,* means white person or foreigner, particularly those from Europe and other Western countries.

When God Speaks

Hunting Day

The shaping of such a leader takes time, prayer, and investment. It's not by chance that this charismatic leader was born into the Kasimba clan as a grandson to the chief. Nor is it an accident that Elijah's clan belongs to the Buganda tribe, the largest of the sixty-plus tribes in Uganda. The wealthiest ethnic group in the nation, its 7.6 million people make up approximately seventeen percent of Uganda's 45 million population.[14] Elijah firmly believes his position in his family, his relationships, and even his specific clan and tribe were divinely arranged to position him for leadership success.

As chief of the Kasimba clan, George William Bakkulumpagi was greatly revered among his community. Elijah describes his grandfather as hardworking, driven, loving, generous, and extremely well-loved by the clan. Elijah's mom also sings his praises.

"My-father-in-law had a special love for me," says Eseza. "I learned to be obedient, loyal, and to serve him and he appreciated my patience. It caught his favor and he took special notice of me. Sometimes he bought me soap when I had nothing to wash with. When I was naked, he would buy clothes. And, my son—he loved Elijah very much."

---

[14] source: http://www.worldatlas.com/articles/largest-ethini-groups-in-uganda.html

When God Speaks

The chief's love for his grandson spilled over into quality time together. Elijah cherishes his childhood memories of hunting days with his grandfather.

*****

Elijah cracks open one eye and sees a dim light has moved into the room. He sits up and peers out a tiny crack in the wall of his grandfather's hut. The sun is just beginning to peek over the swaying grass. He yawns and considers more sleep, then suddenly remembers. He bolts from his palm sleeping mat and looks out the entrance to his grandfather's hut. *Today is hunting day!*

Seven-year-old Elijah has been invited to join the clan hunting expedition. Though the chief has dozens of grandchildren, Elijah has been handpicked. The young boy watches as Kasimba men gather bamboo sticks for wild boar traps and wooden spears for the expedition.

"Ssebukyu, take this!" George William tosses the young warrior a spear as they prepare to leave Bugatto village. Elijah eyes the weapon. Grasping it like the expert clan hunters, he pretends to spear an imaginary wild boar just a few yards away.

George William smiles. "That's it, my son. You are learning well. Now try it with the right hand. For a leader of your caliber, you have to be a person of all seasonings. A powerful warrior must be equipped to fight with either hand."

When God Speaks

Chosen by the Chief

I sit with Elijah as he reminisces about his childhood. His winning smile—possibly the widest I've ever seen—cannot be contained at the mention of George William. "My grandfather told me that my mother was the most patient person he'd ever known. Because of that, I got to spend a lot of time with him, much more than all my siblings. I was my grandfather's best friend," he says. In fact, George William so greatly cherished Elijah and Eseza, they were moved into his hut by his specific request. This gave the chief opportunities to give Elijah extra time and attention.

A strong disciplinarian, his devotion for Elijah was often communicated through beatings rather than hugs. "My grandfather would often beat me, giving me many strokes. He was teaching me and warning me about the dangers of certain lifestyles. "He told me never to test any alcohol. He would also point to my father, who had twelve wives, and say 'never be a polygamist like him.'"

Despite George William's addiction to alcohol, Elijah paid close attention to his grandfather's advice. The chief was a heavy drinker and was involved in other cultural traditions that were sinful, but his family and community loved him. "My grandfather was so loving and kind," Elijah remembers. "He was very hard working and very generous. People considered him to be morally upright and they admired him. Excessive drinking was part of our culture and a man of his stature participated in many traditions involving alcohol." The over-drinking wasn't thought of as wrong. Instead, he was quite highly regarded. The chief also disapproved of *any* of his children drinking local brew or other alcohol. "His warning protected me from taking alcohol. I have never tested it and I never will," says Elijah.

In Bugatto Village, it was not uncommon for people to call themselves Christians (because they believed in God) while simultaneously engaging in binge drinking, idol worship, and polygamy.[15] "In my country, if you say a person is a 'Christian,' it doesn't mean that they have a relationship with Jesus Christ. We have 'Christians' on every corner who attend church regularly. But being a born-again Christian is a *big* deal, and not as common. So my grandfather was a heavy drinker, but he went to church and was a 'Christian.'" He also participated in ancestral and demon worship. The chicken-on-the-roof naming ceremony is an example of such a tradition.

Tradition is one thing, but demon worship and witchcraft wreaked havoc in the lives of Elijah's family. The pastor shakes his head as he recalls the horrors of growing up in a culture seeping with witchcraft. "It caused so much trouble. It disturbed me . . . disturbed me and my siblings so deeply."

*****

"Ssebukyu, go fetch some water, please." Eseza's tattered dress was sweat-soaked. She had worked since sun-up preparing a feast for the evening's

---

[15] This seemingly hypocritical lifestyle is common in Ugandan culture. In such societies where religion was introduced by colonists, the line of acceptable behaviors was often blurred by cultural traditions. Before Christianity was brought to Uganda, polygamy, worship of ancestral spirits using shrines and idols, and other traditional practices were widespread. As Christianity grew with the influx of missionaries in the 1800's, some of these practices diminished. However, many deeply-rooted traditions remained, including those involving excessive drinking, fornication, mutilation, etc.

When God Speaks

ceremony. As Elijah carried the *jerrican*[16] to the river, he muttered to himself under his breath, "I don't want to go to the ceremony. Strange things happen."

Yesterday, his grandmother, Erese Nankula, instructed his mother to slaughter several goats and hens for the feast. Eseza and her daughters began cooking *matooke*, millet,[17] rice, and beans before the sun rose. By sunset, the meal was finally ready.

As darkness set in, Elijah's stomach tightened. He dreaded watching as the food his mommy slaved to prepare was given away to gods. The bizarre chanting, howling, and dancing made his skin crawl. It felt more like a death parade than a celebration. But, for some reason, his grandmother insisted his family attend.

Ugandan witch doctor. Picture: AFP Source: AFP

The sound of maracas signaled the start of the "worship" time. As clan members chanted in unison, Elijah watched his grandmother Erese's face contort into strange expressions. *Is that my*

---

[16] plastic flat-sided container for liquids, usually holding about 5 US gallons or approximately 20 liters.

[17] a nutritious grain, found in certain regions of Africa, that is harvested and ground into flour to make bread. Millet is also used to make alcohol.

grandmother? She began chanting strange sounding words, calling out names of various demons and evil spirits.

Then she spoke very clearly: "I have not come alone." Erese's mouth formed the words, but it wasn't his grandmother's voice. Elijah closed his eyes tightly and hid behind his mother. "I have come with . . ." As the voice spoke names of spirits, she transformed from a shrunken, old woman to an energetic, sprite young lady. She began singing and dancing like a professional.

Elijah shot a look of panic at his brother. They read each other's minds: *Grandmother never dances.* In fact, friends always teased the reserved woman, trying to convince her to dance at weddings and other celebrations, but she refused.

This can't be my grandmother. It looks like her, but it's not her. She would never act so foolishly. Elijah's confusion mounted.

Erese ran in circles around the chicken coop and then began to jump—high. So high, she was able to reach the roofs of the village huts. Still panting from her gymnastics, she ran up next to Elijah, who stood trembling behind his mother. He didn't want the strange woman anywhere near him or his family.

"Eseza," a man's voice instructed Elijah's mother, but it was Erese's lips that formed the words. "We are hungry. Feed us, now!" With shaking hands, Elijah's mom lugged large gourds full of beans, rice and the goat meat she had slaughtered and cooked earlier that day.

The old-woman-turned-young gobbled the food. Within seconds, it vanished. Elijah was dumbfounded how his gaunt grandmother, who barely ate two helpings of beans a day, had devoured food in a flash that took an entire day to prepare.

"We are still hungry," Erese moaned. With rice and beans still in her mouth, the demon-possessed woman pointed to a nearby goat tied to a tree. "That animal over there—go kill that goat!"

Eseza turned to fetch the goat, but then hesitated. The owner of the goat hadn't given permission to slaughter it. Stalling, she wiped her sweaty hands on her dress.

"What's wrong with you, woman?! You don't want to slaughter that goat? But we are hungry. We will just do it then—" All at once, the goat lay dead, with the skin and head removed. Horrified, Elijah gasped and masked his eyes from the bloody scene. He wanted to scream, but he held his breath and took refuge behind his mother's dress.

*****

The demonic horrors Elijah endured are not unusual in Uganda. Children at both Hands of Love orphanages commonly report such disturbing encounters which cause bouts of panic, anxiety, and nightmares. Elijah strives to combat ignorance and educate Western missionaries wanting to help serve at the orphanages. "It's very important for those who wish to visit our country, to understand these problems of witchcraft and devil worship. Satan uses ignorance and would like churches to be ignorant of scripture and the existence of demons. As I travel the world, I meet many who don't believe that demons exist. That is trouble. My family and I have suffered from these demons. Many whom we serve have suffered too."

Sowing Leaders

Serving the suffering is part of a pastor's job. But Elijah didn't always know he was going to be a pastor. God called him into this role through his mother's prayers, encouraging words, and by seeds planted by influential people. "My maternal grandfather, Eriahzali Gunju, was a pastor. He used to tell me I would be a church leader. It wasn't something I'd ever thought of or even desired. Whenever he said it, I would dismiss the thought. But the idea began to develop in me further beginning at age six."

As Elijah grew, the leadership seed planted by his grandfather took root. "That notion of being a church leader grew in me. Whenever I would see national church leaders, something would speak to me: *You are going to be like them.* I would hear them speaking English. This encouraged me to work harder on my education."

Not surprisingly, Elijah was chosen at an early age to be the Head Prefect of the preschool section at his primary school. Beginning at age five, students were selected to perform this job of overseeing children. "Because of tribalism in my country, there was a lot of fighting in the schools. As Head Prefect, it was my role to oversee kids ages five to twelve years, and if I found any child that was fighting, I was expected to intervene. If there was a big occasion, I was expected to take leadership of those kids," he explains. "When

When God Speaks

I was eight years old, I was appointed as a leader in the church. I began reading the Bible out loud every Sunday."

Ultimately, an inheritance from his paternal grandfather enabled Elijah to fully embrace his destiny as a leader. The day these privileges were awarded, Elijah took a crucial step in his journey of becoming a powerful, visionary leader.

Declared Heir

A robust hunter, seventy-eight-year-old George William set out for a hunting expedition with nine others. This time, without young Elijah. Carrying spears and nets and scantily-dressed in animal hides, the hunting attendants accompanied the chief. Later that day, as Eseza prepared *matooke* for their evening meal, a loud movement in the bush rattled her. She stood to get a better view and glimpsed a formation of spears bobbing just above the tall bush grasses, like a school of fish moving along the ocean's surface. The expedition had returned unusually early. Her father-in-law, laid out on a hide, was being carried by two strong men. The chief's eyes were closed and his face, pale. Eseza braced herself for the inevitable.

The families of the Kasimba clan knew his last days were fast approaching. The next morning, George William convened his closest family, and read his will. As his last wishes were shared, looks of disappointment and grief flashed across several faces. Elijah's father looked especially out of sorts. He disagreed with the decision to appoint Elijah, not himself, as the chief's heir.

When God Speaks

Eseza tried not to gloat but inside, she was beaming. She knew why Elijah had been chosen. The God of the impossible had heard her prayers.

*****

"This news didn't go well with my father," Elijah says, "because it meant that all my grandfather's property was coming into my name. That caused big trouble. It was also a problem for my other relatives and some of my stepmothers because I was not the oldest boy. The second wife of my father had an older son. But I was declared the heir. Little did I know that God would later use part of that inheritance to bless millions of people—the land we are using now for Hands of Love."

"For a person such as the Chief to appoint me and my son?" Eseza says. "That meant he trusted me. That was God's providence for so many things. My father-in-law appreciated my patience. That is partly why he chose my son to be heir. He said, 'I have no gift to give you. Let me appoint your son to be heir.' He even appointed me to take care of his wife[18] and all his property. That was a *big* honor. Yes, that was God's providence. God is the Owner of everything. The Planner of everything. We are not able to do anything, but He is able to do everything."

Tribal Ceremony

We are in "the sticks." As my husband Dan, Elijah, and I drive into the tiny corner of Bugatto village where Elijah grew up, I spot an elderly woman seated

---

[18] Elijah's grandfather was a serial monogamist. He had more than one wife, but only one wife at a time.

When God Speaks

by a mud hut. "That one is my aunt." He points and smiles. It has been too long since their last reunion.

"Auntie" greets us warmly with a beautiful smile. We are introduced with a triplet of handshakes and Lugandan small talk translated to English, compliments of Elijah. A gold-and-magenta-dyed, hand-woven palm mat provides a stunning buffer between her knees and the dirt. Her humble posture wins us instantly. It signals kindness, respect, and deference.

Next, the old woman escorts our entourage down a dirt path. Elijah leads the expedition, which consists of a motley mélange of *wazungu*, villagers, and bush children. Moments ago, we doled out a bag of bubble gum to beautiful, grubby-faced kids who appeared out of nowhere—dozens of them. They follow close on our heels, like ants on a honey trail. As we walk, Elijah reaches over to grab hold of a skinny boy's hand. His gaunt frame is leaner than anyone would like. His tiny hand disappears in the pastor's large grasp.

We arrive at the family burial ground, which looks more like a vegetable garden than a cemetery. If Auntie hadn't pointed it out, we would have walked right over Chief George William Bakkulumpagi's resting place. Elijah leans up against the twisted trunk of a massive tree. The soft, papery bark of this bark cloth tree is still used by village mothers to swaddle their newborns. On this very ground, his clan assembled in August of 1978 for a monumental ceremony. What took place on that day sealed Elijah's destiny and dramatically changed the course of his life.

When God Speaks

Auntie points to the tree, chatters to Elijah, then points some more. He turns and translates. Old stories, tales and memories become new as he relays her comments to the group. Auntie fills in details Elijah has forgotten.

*****

The day had come to make sure young Elijah is the true heir. His father and mother, assorted family members, and a smattering of clan officials encircled a large pot of boiling water. They held their breath as Elijah's umbilical cord[19] was placed in the scalding water-herb mixture. According to custom, if the cord failed to float, his identity and position as heir to the chief would be questioned. The crowd waited, staring at the shriveled cord. After three silent minutes, it was still afloat. Elijah was indeed the grandson and appointed heir of Chief George William. Eseza breathed a sigh of relief and offered a silent prayer of thanks.

Next, hoards of Kasimba clan members began arriving. They came from far and wide to pay respects at Chief George William Bakkulumpagi's Last Funeral Rites. Thousands gathered in Bugatto Village for one week of mourning, ceremonies, and feasts.

Eseza was consumed with preparations for the funeral and other important events. Though morning hadn't yet broken, a flurry of activity stirred as the village visitors awakened.

---

[19] A Baganda tradition, the umbilical cord is saved from birth and retained for later use in traditional ceremonies. source: http://www.everyculture.com/wc/Tajikistan-to-Zimbabwe/Baganda.html#ixzz3HOsQs1o2

When God Speaks

"Today is the day, Ssebukyu. Time to get up!" At five a.m., his mother stood over him smiling. In her right hand, she held a sharp knife. "Sit up and be still." The boy rubbed his eyes, sat up, and froze as she began shaving his head. The young heir-in-waiting yawned as Eseza carefully wielded the knife. She prayed a blessing as his wiry black hair succumbed to the blade.

Elijah ran his hand over his smooth head and exhaled. He knew it was a big day and hoped he wouldn't mess up. Remembering his mother's prayers helped him breathed a little easier.

Next, Eseza dressed nine-year-old Elijah in bark cloth[20], the traditional choice

Ugandan women wearing barkcloth dress

for those in mourning. She took her son's hand and led him out of the hut to join George William's family. A huge throng of bark-cloth-clad tribe members were assembled in front of the chief's hut. The mourners wailed loudly out of respect for this important and beloved man. They ran, crying and screaming, away from the hut, chasing the spirit of death into a nearby swamp.

The loud cries and wailing rattled the skinny boy, but Eseza's firm grip steadied him. He watched the mourners and recalled precious time spent with

---

[20] A fibrous material made by beating sodden strips of the inner bark of bark cloth trees.

his grandfather hunting, digging in the garden, and sitting by the fire. His mother brushed a tear from his cheek. "I will miss him too, Ssebukyu."

The next few hours were a blur for the young heir. He had many responsibilities, including blessing the animals waiting to be slaughtered for tonight's feast. At last, it was time for the main ceremony, where he would assume his position as clan chief.

Though his heart raced, the soon-to-be-chief bravely took his place in the center of an enormous crowd gathered beneath the bark cloth tree. They swayed to the steady thumping of drums. The clan elder gestured toward a small chair draped in a spotted genet[21] hide, the Kasimba clan mascot. Elijah settled into it while Eseza took another seat close by.

An elder approached Elijah holding George William's spear. The crowd fell silent as his young fingers took hold of the weapon. The weight of the moment pressed down on Elijah . . . he exhaled and touched each pointy tip of the twelve-headed spear. The spear signified authority and leadership. Though the one holding it was young, he now possessed the right to lead the entire clan.

genet

---

[21] Cat-like animal with a pale grey and black-spotted coat, with a long striped tail, common to rural areas of East Africa. (source: http://en.wikipedia.org/wiki/Common_genet)

When God Speaks

Eseza couldn't contain her joy. She reveled in the turning-point moment, whispering thanks. *God, You have blessed him. Thank You, God, for hearing our prayers. I know You are answering us. Please, God, let him be the leader You are calling him to be. Give him all that he needs and deliver him from evil.*

Eseza's silent prayer was interrupted by two men who approached Elijah with a large bag. Voices screeched and reeled into staccatos of tribal chants. The men dragged the bulky, bark cloth bag and gladly put it to rest with a thud beside Elijah.

Though the bag was tied shut, Eseza knows what's inside. The ancestral spirits passed down through her father-in-law's family line were about to be passed to Elijah. Under her breath, she ticked her tongue. Recognizing the familiar voice, the young chief glanced over at his mom.

He froze. Eseza's gaze was riveted on Elijah. She began to blink both eyes. Open. Shut. Open. Shut.

Elijah examined the sack. The clan holy man (witch doctor) opened it and began removing a collection of carved wooden idols: first a monkey skull, then a snakeskin . . . But, as he extended the monkey skull to Elijah, the young boy's hand remained at his side. Elijah lowered his gaze. Out of the corner of his eye, he glimpsed Eseza, who continued to blink[22].

---

[22] Blinking both eyes repeatedly signals to a Ugandan what shaking a head and clicking a tongue communicates to an American: no, no, no!

Infuriated, the holy man glared at Eseza. He and everyone else knew what she has silently signaled to her son: don't accept the idols. Each of the idols represented an ancestor, which the heir is obligated to worship. Making sacrifices and performing bizarre acts to appease deceased ancestors would go hand in hand with accepting the idols. Chaotic shouts erupted among the on-lookers, but Eseza remained calm and stoic.

By refusing the spirits, Eseza protected Elijah from 363 ways for evil to influence his life. Once again, the God of the impossible had intervened to save her son from destruction.

Consecrated

Though Eseza's controversial gesture wreaked havoc among the village that day, Elijah remains eternally grateful for his mother's courage and stubbornness. "My grandfather instructed my mother to refuse those spirits because each one had tortured him. Many people tried to persuade her otherwise, but she refused to allow evil spirits access to my life."

"Many questioned how a young boy, just nine years old, could decline these important objects," Elijah says. "That day, I became the heir, but 363 ancestral spirits from my grandfather were passed to another man. Until his recent death, that man has always been a devil worshiper."

Elijah reflects on that turning point and praises pour forth. "I think about that moment and I cry. That is how God protected me and protected His resources and His potential in me. God's plans are the best. Truly, God has big

When God Speaks

plans for His people! Plans for good and not for bad, to give us a future and a hope[23]. God used my mother at that time. That was a big thing—one of the most significant things that has ever happened to me. It was that year when God chose me to be totally consecrated for Him."

God sets before each of us a choice, just as he set a choice before Eseza and Elijah that day—the choice of death or life. We are given the option to bring destruction or blessing:

> *"This day I call heaven and earth as witnesses against you that I have set before you life and death, blessings and curses. Now choose life, so that you and your children may live and that you may love the Lord your God, listen to His voice and hold fast to Him" (Deuteronomy 30:19-20).*

Though he refused the idols, not all symbolic gifts were refused by the young heir. "An Anglican pastor was at the ceremony who handed a Bible over to me. That, I gladly received," Elijah says. "And, even though I refused the spirits, I remained the heir with honor and received my grandfather's property. My mother warned many friends that I received the property and position, but I never received the power to preside over traditional ceremonies as the chief."

"God is God! He used my mother to protect me. By becoming heir, I was awarded a lot of land and some of this property is turning into income for

---

[23] Jeremiah 29:11

our ministry. In certain parts of Uganda, land is more expensive than in the United States, because of our country's overpopulation. With land fragmentation and the increased cost of living and education, demands are very high for land today." The gift of inheriting his grandfather's land was indeed a tremendous blessing that continues to sustain and prosper thousands of kids.

Inheriting a Kingdom

That August day, under the bark cloth tree, God not only chose an heir, but launched Elijah into full-time leadership—a leader who would influence many others to choose life and become heirs. But these yet-to-be heirs would not inherit the Kasimba clan. Theirs would be a different kingdom:

> *"But Jesus called for them, saying, "Permit the children to come to Me, and do not hinder them, for the kingdom of God belongs to such as these" (Luke 18:16).*

Each Hands of Love child is given the opportunity to know and become an heir to the Most High King. For those who choose Him, theirs is an inheritance far surpassing any earthly possession. To such as these belongs the kingdom of God.

> *"So, you are no longer a slave, but God's child; and since you are his child, God has made you also an heir" (Galatians 4:7).*

When God Speaks

When God Speaks

Starfish and Pebbles

"Once upon a time, there was a wise man who used to go to the ocean to do his writing. He had a habit of walking on the beach before he began his work. One day, as he was walking along the shore, he looked down the beach and saw a human figure moving like a dancer. He smiled to himself at the thought of someone who would dance to the day, and so he walked faster to catch up.

As he got closer, he noticed that the figure was that of a young man, and what he was doing was not dancing at all. The young man was reaching down to the shore, picking up small objects, and throwing them into the ocean. He came closer still and called out "Good morning! May I ask what you are doing?"

The young man paused, looked up, and replied, "Throwing starfish into the ocean."

"I must ask, then, why are you throwing starfish into the ocean?" asked the somewhat-startled wise man.

To this, the young man replied, "The sun is up and the tide is going out. If I don't throw them in, they'll die."

Upon hearing this, the wise man commented, "But, young man, do you not realize that there are miles and miles of beach and there are starfish all along every mile? You can't possibly make a difference!"

When God Speaks

At this, the young man bent down, picked up yet another starfish, and threw it into the ocean. As it met the water, he said, "It made a difference for that one." —by Loren Eiseley

*****

If you walked onto a beach strewn with thousands of starfish would you walk on by? Or, would you stop and throw one or two back in the ocean? It might cost you a few moments of time on the beach, but by sacrificing five minutes, you'd make a tangible difference.

Pastor Elijah and others could be easily overwhelmed by the staggering odds Ugandans are up against. According to the 12th Annual Joint AIDS Review (July 2018- June 2019) the AIDS burden in Uganda is 1,400,000 infections[24]. Considering the behemoth epidemic, it's understandable why people flee Uganda for greener pastures. Highly-educated Ugandans frequently fall prey to this temptation.

The starfish-tossing young man and Pastor Elijah have chosen a different path. Instead of jumping ship, they roll up their sleeves. "Every one of us can do something," Elijah says, "and eventually . . . eventually . . . the work will be done."

Believe me, I am tempted to check out, change the channel or continue down the beach, rather than confront the problem. I've almost succumbed to

---

[24] source: http://uas.go.ug/content/12th-jar-report-2019

that myself. Hearing of Uganda's tribal violence, starvation, and unthinkable acts against children made me want to curl up in a corner and cry.

But, after drying your tears, why not extend your hand, and pick up a starfish— and toss it back into the water? It may not cure 1,400,000 cases of AIDS, but it might initiate a mustard seed of change, and eventually the work will be done.

Skyla Campbell is a hand extender. A friend showed fourteen-year-old Skyla pictures of Rwandan orphans who were desperately in need. Rather than ignoring the ache in her heart, she extended a hand by making some phone calls to area stores. Her efforts snowballed and, soon, twenty-five companies agreed to make in-kind donations.

Skyla refused to ignore the problem. Now, children in more than fifteen countries have received art and school supplies, toys, shirts, and shoes. Her one act of love of a phone call rippled into *Operation Global Impact (OGI)*, an international ministry that includes a blog and Facebook page and has grabbed the attention of media in several cities around the nation. She hopes the ministry will one day swell into a non-profit organization.

Operation Global Impact has ministered to folks in Burundi, the Philippines, China, Tanzania, Rwanda, Uganda, and Mali. After organizing a Barnes and Noble book fair, OGI raised $1,000 for a school in Ethiopia. The ministry recently secured a donation from Dell for five laptops. OGI will oversee shipping the computers to Uganda.

When God Speaks

People like Pastor Elijah and Skyla get it. They grasp the profound truth of Mahatma Gandhi's famous mantra: "The best way to find yourself is to lose yourself in the service of others." In the process of losing herself, Skyla found her *want to*. "I've truly found myself—my passion. I've found what I want to do for the rest of my life."

Skyla is not discouraged by the small scope of her work. She is simply throwing one starfish at a time back into the ocean. But she knows it makes a difference to *that one*.

"Are we ending poverty?" Skyla asks. "No. Are we going to give everyone on the planet clean water? No. Are we going to provide everyone with a house and free medical access? No. What we can do is bring smiles to children. Remembering those smiles keeps me focused. It is kind of our whole purpose in being here. Do what you can, where you are. Bring small moments of joy to other people."

What about you? Have you recently seen or heard something that caused a soul-deep crack? Begin by asking God, *what do you want me to do*? If you don't hear a response, keep praying. Elijah prayed and fasted for close to a year before God spelled out his calling. Because of Elijah's obedience and 298 days of waiting on God's answer, thousands of children's lives are forever changed for the good.

And because of hand extenders like Skyla Campbell, children in Rwanda are smiling.

When God Speaks

It all begins with an open hand and a simple prayer . . . *Lord, what do you want me to do?*

4

Through the Dust
The Power of Education

It is jostling, dusty business, traveling the rocky roads of the Kayunga District where Elijah grew up. Our driver, Stephen, expertly navigates our SUV over the rain-ravaged roads the wet season has left behind. The tires kick up a terracotta haze as we pass the swamp where Elijah was born.

"This brings new meaning to the scripture, 'He lifts the poor from the dust and the needy from the garbage dump[25],'" I say to Pastor Elijah seated next to me.

"Oh my friend . . ." Elijah shakes his head, "just look behind us." I glance out the back window of our truck. Squinting, I scan the dust cloud and barely make out two shoeless figures walking: a woman and child wearing dirt from head to toe. Out the side window, the corn stalks are dressed in red like a snow-caked pine in a New England blizzard.

Arriving at *Kayonza Church of Uganda Primary School* where Elijah completed his elementary education, we are greeted by 1,056 beautiful—albeit dusty—students. Dressed in green threadbare uniforms, they settle down, sitting

---

[25] 1 Samuel 2:8

criss-cross-applesauce on a grassy knoll in front of the successful national leader. They listen wide-eyed and barefooted as Elijah shares the story of his first pair of shoes. His words drip with inspiration.

"All of you here are not wearing shoes. That is not your fault. You don't need to feel sorry for yourselves. I didn't have shoes until I was fifteen years old. I got my first blanket when I was thirteen. That means, I went through *this* school without shoes. During primary school, I don't remember putting on a full pair of shorts, but wore only rags. I'm not ashamed to talk about it. So, when you look at your friend putting on a torn shirt, please don't laugh. That friend may end up being the next president of Uganda."

I watch their eyes brighten with hope as this tall, articulate Ugandan pastor speaks life into their tattered, hungry lives. Countless enemies, not the least of which is abject poverty, leave them thirsty for encouragement. They drink in his words.

"Some of you have parents, but some may have none. Some in your families have died of HIV/AIDS." Disease, sexual promiscuity, tribal fighting, cannibalism, child sacrifice—rank after rank—an army of cultural evils assaults Uganda's youth, threatening to annihilate their future.

"But let me tell you who will change all this. It is not the prime minister of Uganda. It is not even our President. Elijah Sebuchu will not change Uganda," he confesses, laying a hand on his heart. "Your teacher will not change this nation. Touch the hand of your neighbor and say: *It is YOU who will change this nation.*"

When God Speaks

A frail-looking girl, seated in the front row of children, studies the dust beneath her as his words settle in. "I grew up from the dust," he continues. "You can make it! It is only a matter of time. You will get your shoes! You are just passing through this!" His deep voice echoes through the school yard, swelling as it reverberates off the crumbling brick school buildings.

He squats down, firmly takes hold of the girl's slight frame, then whisks her up into long arms that are tailor made for hugging children. "Look at this child! God has the power to lift up everyone of you." He holds her high above her friends as the students erupt into joyful chuckles.

A tiny smirk emerges, then morphs into a full-blown smile on her face. She no longer stares at the dirt. The once shoeless, now smartly dressed pastor in a striped business shirt and dress shoes has come to speak at her school today. He has raised her up, lifting both her spirits and her sights. Her gaze shifts out over the heads of her classmates: the future presidents, pilots, and pastors of Uganda.

"I want you to know that I am your fellow pupil." He lowers her back down to the red earth. She plants both feet, stands a little straighter, and rivets her gaze on Elijah. His gentle, intense eyes and warm smile collaborate, refusing to let any child miss the encouragement. "I went through the dust that you are going through. Today, I have traveled to many different parts of the world. I've been to America many times, to African and European countries. I have sat before the president of this nation, the vice president, both small and big people. So if God made a way for me, He can make a way for anyone."

When God Speaks

Holding Light

Elijah Sebuchu firmly believes that education will raise Uganda's vulnerable children from the dust. It's the key to unlocking future success, empowering them to break the downward cycle of poverty.

"Whenever I get the chance to speak to children, I tell them: Study very hard! Read books! Because a good education will empower them to compete with people all over the world. Uganda needs educated people."

For decades, young Ugandans have encountered a plethora of socioeconomic and cultural barriers to education. In Bugatto Village, out of necessity, impoverished families kept their children home from school to hunt. Many preteen girls were denied an education. Instead, they were prepared for marriage and given away beginning as early as age eleven. Other parents weren't willing to risk their children's lives for the sake of education. Threats of wild animal attacks, child sacrifice, and even severe flooding in the rainy season convinced them to safeguard their children at home.

But thanks in large part to a mother who breathed the importance of learning into her son, Elijah was never hindered from receiving an education. That is, barring those rare occasions when he didn't pray loud enough for his mother to hear. School was a lifeline for him, one he firmly grasped from the moment he first set foot in a classroom.

*****

Elijah's four-year-old feet were filthy. He was on mile two of his three-mile walk to join his kindergarten classmates at *Bugonya Church of Uganda Primary*

School. He raked a stick along the dust, making a zigzag trail behind him. He had no books to carry, but the stick would serve as his writing instrument. The dirt would become his "paper" when it came time to practice writing the alphabet later in the school day.

Founded by the Anglican Church, the school was tight on resources. Even so, Elijah couldn't wait to get there. Anxious to begin the very best part of his day, he sped up as soon as he spied the grass-thatched schoolhouse.

Elijah whizzed through his early grades, then attended primary four through seven at *Kayonza Church of Uganda Primary School,* located seven miles from his village. Situated next to a swamp abundant with papyrus, the school attracted families from Southern Sudan. The Sudanese used papyrus for weaving mats to sell for a small but steady income.

At school one day, Elijah sat next to some Bugatto Village kids who shared drinks from a yellow *jerrican* in the hot afternoon sun. The kids from Sudan glared at him from across the school yard. They shot snickering looks at one another, as if they knew a secret about Elijah.

His thirsty lips stuck together. He passed the can, not taking a single sip. Skinny Elijah tried to drink as little water as possible so he wouldn't have to use the pit latrines. He had run into the Sudanese boys there before and it wasn't pretty. His grandfather had warned him: "Those Sudanese are fighters." *He's got that right,* Elijah thought. *Fighters who like to pick on the skinniest one in their grade.*

When God Speaks

He watched the other children gulp their drinks and he couldn't stand it any longer. Grabbing hold of the can, Elijah drank deep. Though the water tasted foul, he didn't know the difference. It was wet and that was all he cared about. He wiped his mouth and passed the can to his neighbor. Later that day, the urge came, and he hurried to the latrine. The familiar pang in his stomach wasn't hunger. It was fear. As he opened the door, a left hook came fast and furious from an angry Sudanese boy. His punch hit Elijah squarely on his lower jaw. As the youngest and leanest in his grade, it didn't take much to drop him to the dirt.

Elijah was still coming to when he heard a scuffle. He managed to open one eye long enough to see two huge feet standing in front of him. There was only one other student with feet that large. *Thank God. It's Godfrey!* With little effort, Elijah's older and bigger brother catapulted the bully out of the latrine, onto his back.

"Don't ever mess with him again," Godfrey shouted. "Go beat up someone your own size, or you will deal with me!"

Though Elijah's size didn't win him any fights, his intelligence won him favor with the students, which helped him advance as a leader. At age eleven, while other boys from his village were at home hunting, he was elected the Kayonza school timekeeper. One year later, he and three others were chosen by their peers as head prefects. Similar to a student council officer, Elijah served as head prefect for two years. These leadership opportunities were divine stepping stones guiding him toward God's calling. Beginning with the chicken named Ssebukyu, each experience furthered his grooming into the "warrior" leader.

"I studied very hard and was always at the top of my class. I was not a perfect student, though. I had trouble like any other child. Some of my teachers used to cane me. But I learned to appreciate them because they helped me become a better pupil. For this reason, I often tell young people: 'Listen to your teachers! Whenever they cane you, they are teaching you. You will be very foolish if you don't follow them and very wise if you listen and obey them, as long as they are good. These teachers, they are holding light before you. They are helping to lift you up.'

"I have forgotten some of my teachers' names, but I will never forget their work in me. Some of them may not even have a place to live today. I now have a place to live because they invested in *me*."

The Importance of Shoes

For most fifteen year olds—American or Ugandan—appearance matters. Acceptance is critical for teenagers and wardrobe largely impacts the way others perceive them. For Elijah, certain articles of clothing were important for different reasons. In 1984, his father enrolled him in *Kasawo Senior Secondary School-Kigayaza* and provided his son with a mandatory component of the uniform dress code. It was a moment Elijah will never forget.

*****

When God Speaks

"Ssebukyu, I have something for you." Eseza called for her son. She was grinning from ear to ear, her hands tucked behind her. She had rehearsed this moment for weeks. After all, for fifteen years she had waited to give him such a gift.

"Yes, Mommy." The boy stood in front of his mother, towering a good six inches above her.

"Your father purchased these for you." Eseza placed a pair of simple, cloth shoes on the ground in front of him.

He looked at the shoes and then at his mother. Blank faced, he blinked and stared at her while the reality of her gift settled in. He picked her up and swung her around and around. Dizzy laughter and joy filled the mud hut.

"Are you going to try them on? Or, are you going to dance with your mom?"

Elijah took the shoes in his hands and carefully examined them. He lifted them to his nose and inhaled. He slipped them on and walked around, but the oversized shoes fit more like flip-flops than loafers. Elijah didn't care. They were his first pair of shoes and he would wear them with pride.

With or Without Shoes

"That year, I put on shoes for the first time. I will never forget that moment. It was a *very* big deal for me," he says, "even though they were grossly oversized."

When God Speaks

Elijah's father intentionally purchased the shoes several sizes larger than needed to prevent his son from out growing them too quickly.

The shoes made for a quirky morning routine, but one Elijah happily adopted in exchange for the immense privilege of owning them. "Every morning I would stuff the toes with some pieces of newspaper. Since we owned no towels to dry ourselves, I would bathe, and with soaking wet feet, I put on the shoes with the paper stuffed into them."

One year later, a fellow classmate gave Elijah an old towel which slightly augmented his routine. "That was the first time I used a towel. My routine became to bathe and dry with my friend's old towel, then stuff the wet towel and an old rag into my shoes. Whenever I share this experience with my own children, they always laugh!"

On a national radio program, Elijah was given the opportunity to share this and other details of his life story. The series aired for ten weeks and the ripple effects of the broadcast were staggering. Several million Ugandans tuned in to hear the details of how a prominent national leader awkwardly trudged around his middle school in giant shoes. Callers identified with his many struggles and were inspired to rise above challenges with God's help, regardless of whether they owned shoes.

Attending Kasawo School won Elijah other comforts. "My father somehow managed to get a one-inch mattress for me, which was also required by the boarding school. That was the first time I slept on a mattress. It was so thin, I could still feel the floor, but it was better than sleeping on the ground, as I had done my entire life."

The Face of Brutality

While Elijah was successfully navigating his school years, Idi Amin ruled Uganda in an eight year "reign of terror" as president. His notoriously grisly, tyrannical ways earned Amin the nickname, "The Butcher of Uganda." Out of the country's total population of twelve million, an estimated 300,000 of his opponents were killed and countless others were tortured and imprisoned as a result of his brutal leadership. Elijah's village and even his family were among those who succumbed to the flagrant violence.

"Amin's soldiers invaded villages throughout the Kayunga District. They were beating our people, killing some and raping others—horrible things," Elijah remembers. "When I was eight years old, they invaded my father's home and raped six of my father's wives. This happened as I sat watching the entire scene. That experience troubled me for many years. It was a great shock to witness that."

"Another time, as I was walking home from school, some of these men chased me. They were going to kill me, but a man from my village intervened and saved me." The man hid Elijah in a nearby building until the soldiers retreated.

When God Speaks

Caught in the crossfire of military unrest[26], Kayunga District and the surrounding region were declared a danger zone. "It was nearly impossible to walk for even five minutes without encountering soldiers or a dead body. It was horrible. These men would do whatever they wanted. They would rape girls and women. The rebel groups wanted young boys. They were in high demand. They would capture and take them into the bush to join the guerrillas. If you came across rebels they might do anything with you, including kill you. Government soldiers would capture boys to be in the looting crew. If the boys refused, they would be killed. Otherwise, they were forced to break into people's homes."

To be poor and hungry was one thing, but such violent encounters with soldiers ushered in an almost unbearable chapter of Elijah's childhood. Uganda's volatile political climate turned his should-be innocent years into the stuff nightmares are made of.

child soldier
Source: the Rising Continent

"The soldiers were so notorious. They were extremely brutal, especially in the raping of my father's wives. Seeing this troubled me deeply. It instilled such a deep fear in me. I experienced nightmares of the bullets that were shot, the people being killed while I watched. Nightmares of seeing women raped, and others bound.

---

[26] In 1979, Amin was dethroned by Ugandan nationalists, resulting in government unrest and widespread military invasions. Between 1981 and 1985, another estimated 300,000 of Uganda's civilians died as guerrillas, known as the National Resistance Army, battled Milton Obote's government forces, the Uganda National Liberation Army.

When God Speaks

Even people's heads being chopped off. For me, up until this day, I still have trouble when I hear loud noises. That is how I grew up. You're in the bush and you hear the bullets ringing. And this happens constantly, not just for one day, or one week, or one year."

The Day Death Walked In

Elijah Sebuchu is a man who has stared death in the face and walked away more times than he can count. But of all his struggles, his bouts with disease, starvation, homelessness, and even lions, perhaps Elijah's most harrowing and closest encounter with death occurred in 1985. His father's Bugatto home was again looted by government soldiers. Later that day, rebels visited his boarding school and captured four hundred students. Though he was not one of the four hundred, the events to come would make him wish he were.

*****

"Line up there!" The soldier pointed to the concrete wall. "Now, you dogs. Now! Go!" He barked at the children like they had all done something horribly wrong. But they hadn't. Rebel leader, Yoweri Museveni had ordered the capture of 400 students. The angry soldiers, sent as a gesture of retaliation by President Milton Obote, barked orders at Elijah and his classmates. The frightened students were caught between the brutal and bloody disagreement of two military forces.

Elijah stared in shock at the grimacing soldier's gun. It was pointing directly at him. "Move, boy!"

When God Speaks

He hustled to the wall and stood frozen next to his classmates. The girls, who stood upright against the concrete wall, whimpered quietly. Their frail bodies shook with tiny sobs as they awaited the next order. As their silent tears fell, Elijah's hatred toward the soldiers grew.

The soldier reached down to adjust his shoe. His gun pointed to the ground.

Now's my chance to run, he thought. But the moment Elijah inched his foot out of line, the soldier stood up again, eyeing him suspiciously.

"You! What do you think you are doing? You want to get your head blown off!" The soldier began to laugh. His wicked cackling made fifteen-year-old Elijah want to cry for his mom. Instead, he inched his foot back against the wall and looked straight ahead. The soldier turned away and Elijah quietly exhaled in relief.

Another soldier approached the end of the line and began counting the row of students. When he reached the end, he overheard both men confirming their counts: 227.

Perhaps it was by the grace of God that no warning came.

A deafening cadence reverberated throughout the school yard.

Ratattat . . . ratattat . . . ratattat!

Waves of screaming came next.

Another cadence of gunfire.

soldiers barking orders,

children whimpering,

feet shuffling,

and more shouting.

And then, just as suddenly as the gunfire commenced, it ended.

A deadly silence blanketed the school campus and community.

Elijah's heart pounded, he breathed short, panicky puffs of air. At some point between the gunfire's beginning and end, he fell to the ground. He lay frozen, his right cheek pressed to the red dirt floor, fearing the soldiers' return. Dazed and shaken, he wanted to examine his throbbing right arm for a wound, but didn't dare draw attention to himself. He hadn't a clue if he had been shot.

"Those of us who were not dead, we laid in the same place for hours. We just laid there . . . in pools of blood . . . paralyzed. We were in a state of complete shock. There was blood everywhere. At some point, I realized I was not wounded. Then I walked fifty-eight miles home."

Severely traumatized by the shooting, Elijah doesn't recall his walk home. When he reached his village, his neighbors and family were not expecting him. They had been told that none from the shooting had survived. "It was a *big* shock for my family to see me at home. All of the 227 students were declared dead, but in fact, twenty-seven survived. Everyone was completely amazed that twenty-seven were alive."

Though overjoyed by the sight of their son, the family grieved other losses. "One of my brothers died there. Another had gone missing and was pronounced dead, but after seven months, he emerged alive. Many times, this brother and I have sat together and discussed this tragic event, but I've never determined where he went. I believe he was in shock. Two more relatives from my clan, distant brothers, were also killed, and one sister."

Elijah's wounds inflicted by that day are deep. The piercing grief of losing fellow students and loved ones yet lingers. The man who lives to love children and to raise them up from the dust is still healing from the day death walked into his school to steal 200 young lives. But his work—his *calling*—to offer new life to children, is a balm that soothes. With time, God's grace, and many hugs from the Hands of Love children, the memories slowly fade.

When God Speaks

Work! Work! Work!

What will never fade is Pastor Elijah Sebuchu's passion for learning. The value his mother passed down to him, he passes down to all children: his own five at home and the 2,600 kids he and his staff educate at Hands of Love.

In Uganda, however, receiving an education doesn't come easy. Its high price tag makes school a financial impossibility for many. It takes an average of $780 annually to educate a high school student in Uganda, which seems minimal to most Americans, who pay approximately $8,750 per year for a high school education. But with 40 percent of its population living on less than $1.25 per day, Uganda is one of the poorest countries in the world. On average, 75% of Ugandan's earn $2,126 annually with 50% of them earning less than $800.00. In contrast, the average American earns $48,672 annually.

As a mother of eleven, Eseza struggled to survive on far less than the average Ugandan. "There was no money to pay for my school fees and uniforms and to feed my family members. Every time we had a school holiday, I worked even more to support myself, my mother and some of my siblings. I cannot remember a job I didn't do. I burned charcoal, carried loads, chopped wood, dug and cleared land, and did laundry for members of different communities. I also traded fish, sold chicken, oranges, jack fruit, and sugarcane. Everything that could bring in money and was acceptable at my age, I would do it."

As Elijah rolled up his sleeves and dug into work and school, he was met with physical threats and other hardships. But abundant blessings seem to greet him at every turn. As God poured out blessings, the young warrior leader began to experience an even greater measure of divine protection in his life. Protection was exactly what Elijah would need as adversity again knocked at his door.

Facing a Beast

Walking along Kampala's roads engages the senses. Dust clouds combat the eyes and the scent of burning charcoal tickles the nose. Most Ugandan's cook with charcoal, which makes it a source of income for others. For Elijah, this smoky smell conjures up an unforgettable confrontation he had as a hard-working, eighteen-year-old student.

"During a holiday break, I left the boarding school I attended to go to a remote location and cut down trees to burn charcoal. I had to walk fifty-eight miles from school to check on the charcoal, because if you let it burn too long, it will turn to ashes."

The grueling walk was not only long, but danger lurked in the dark hours of the early morning. "So, I was walking fifty-eight miles *each way*. At the same time, I was a member of a candidate class, preparing to sit for my national exams[27], to qualify for high school. Because of the time it took to travel the great distance, I had to leave at three a.m. to check on my charcoal, work several days, and then make the long journey back to school."

---

[27] A rigorous standardized test, similar to the SAT, that determines academic aptitude in high school students.

When God Speaks

*****

As young Elijah walked in darkness, he sensed he wasn't alone. The surrounding atmosphere seemed charged by something powerful. His pulse increased. He stopped and listened. Just feet away, he heard the swoosh of the bush grasses, then a low, guttural sound. His blood ran cold. Chills coursed his entire body. Before he could prepare the next logical movement, his adversary appeared.

It was a lion.

His feet froze to the ground. The beast sized up his prey, looking Elijah straight in the eyes, like a prize fighter meeting his underdog challenger. Transfixed by the animal's gaze, Elijah rooted his feet firmly to the ground, allowing no breath to escape for seconds that felt like hours. His soul engaged in a silent prayer.

As suddenly as he had appeared, the lion blinked, turned, and took off. But the young charcoal burner was still not alone.

"There was a man who saw the entire thing." In awe of what he had just witnessed, this man immediately rode his bicycle to seek out a church. "The next day, he gave his life to Christ and eventually became a preacher. He is still a preacher today.

"After meeting the lion, I continued walking fifteen miles, then someone picked me up on a bicycle and saved me from walking the rest of the way."

When God Speaks

Elijah knows it was no mistake that the lion crossed his path in the wee morning hours, at precisely the same time a man in need of God passed by on a bicycle. "That is God!" he punctuates *God,* slapping his leg with an enormous palm. "This lion was yet another thing that was enough to exterminate me from this planet! I indeed praise God for protecting me from that!"

That same year, God used another animal encounter to equip Elijah. Considerably less ferocious, this time *two goats* were indirectly responsible for his continuing education.

Constantine's Goats

To sit for Uganda's national high school entrance exam, there is an extensive registration process. The higher your grade level, the costlier it becomes to register. Unable to afford the costly exam fee, many rising high school students drop out of school.

"The national exam was too expensive for me," Elijah says. "I had no choice but to wait three months. During this time, a relative of one of my father's wives, Mr. Constantine, heard about my situation. He had been following my life for quite some time and heard that I couldn't afford to register for the national exam." Refusing to sit idly by while a promising future leader missed his opportunity, the man extended his hand.

"He was very poor, but he came to me and shared that he had sold two of his goats to pay for me to take the exam. 'Young man,' he told me, 'you are a good leader and you have the potential to become huge in this nation.'

When God Speaks

"Mr. Constantine was a poor man with ninety-six children and at least four wives—perhaps more. Many of his own children never went to school and some dropped out due to lack of money. But this man sold two of his precious goats to bring *me* the money!"

Remembering hushes Elijah—a man rarely at a loss for words—into a humble silence. He shakes his head, closes his eyes and exhales. "This man . . . this man . . . miraculously sacrificed for my education. He brought me the money after riding *many* miles on a bicycle. This was a miracle—this man who gave me the money and said, 'In you, I see potential and a spirit to help other children who may go through what you've been through.'"

Our heavenly Father is still in the miracle business. In God's economy, lions convert men on bicycles and a poor man's goats ripple into a lifetime of education. Hand-extending miracles happen and hearts are captured. Though shaken by shootings and brutality, a skinny, charcoal-selling school boy was becoming the man whose heart God would capture. The God who uses widows' coins, a poor man's goats, and a hungry lion was about to use Elijah as His "hands of love" to rescue Uganda's impoverished and abandoned children.

When God Speaks

The One-Word Prayer

I sat at my laptop, eyes closed, and pictured the dreadful scene in Elijah's school that day. My keyboard clicked as I spelled out the sound of gunfire. R-a-t-t- . . . My cell phone chimed with a text message from my daughter.

> Hi, Mom. Guess where we are.
>
> Where?
>
> Still at the bus stop.
>
> Why?!?
>
> School power and heat are out :(

It's thirty-five degrees outside! My poor thin-blooded Southern children are going to freeze their butts off! I had dropped them off forty minutes ago, but my daughter assured me they were waiting comfortably—and warmly—on the bus. I resumed my writing about the day Elijah can't stand to remember. And then it hit me.

Despite our polar opposite lifestyles, Elijah and I share one thing: our faith in God. Though our needs are vastly different, like kids waiting on a heated

When God Speaks

bus vs. kids waiting days for their next meal, they can look strangely similar. Like the threat of school shootings. In the face of such peril, we cry out with a single word. No other prayer, no other name, has more power than this one word prayer: "Jesus!"

My children's school is located in a reasonably safe area of North Charleston, but neighborhood shootings have, on occasion, happened. Understandably, our school issues a code yellow and immediately locks down the facility at the first hint of a nearby shooting.

Though I am grateful for this security measure, at the end of a code-yellow day, the lock-down efforts aren't what ease my mind. Every week, I gather with a handful of moms for prayer[28]. For sixty minutes, we toss our prayers into an ocean of teenage issues—unplanned pregnancy, suicide, drugs, and school shootings—to ask the all-powerful, sovereign God of the universe to protect our children and our school. *And, oh, by the way, could You please help my son pass his Spanish exam?*

At the end of a code-yellow day, *this* is what settles me down. This hour matters, not because of the ones who pray but because of the One to whom we pray. Though our prayers aren't solely responsible for keeping our school safe, we believe God will guide us through what life may bring and provide protection over us.

---

[28] *Moms in Prayer International* impacts children and schools worldwide for Christ by gathering moms to pray. MIPI's vision is that every school in the world would be covered with prayer. For more information, or to find a group near you, go to www.momsinprayerorg.

When God Speaks

Perhaps Elijah whispered the "Jesus!" prayer the day soldiers entered his school. And the many days he was harbored from evil inside a certain roadside building.

A Safe Haven

Dan, Elijah, and I rode together in silence. I scanned the thirsty Ugandan bush out my side window. The motion of the car and the warm July day joined forces exerting a hypnotic daze over the passengers. Elijah's abrupt instruction to our driver startled me. "Stephen, *mwattu yimilira!*"

The dust kicked up around the car as it came to a quick stop. As the cloud settled, several yards in the distance, a small, whitewashed, concrete building came into view. In contrast to the brightly colored head scarves worn by roadside women balancing baskets of matooke, the building was drab. Elijah fell silent. Eventually, he stepped out of the car and stood there, expressionless, for several minutes. At last, he spoke.

"This was an office building for Kamusabi Parish. While I was in fourth through seventh grades, I passed this place on my walk to school. During those years, I remember being chased by people. They were chasing me and my classmates to catch and sacrifice us. This happened fifty-two times. But whenever we would reach this building, we could hide. A parish chief worked in the building, in addition to one security guard. When we reached this building, our pursuers would give up. The chief and the guard would see us

When God Speaks

coming, welcome us, and offer protection. Once it was safe, we would continue on, running very quickly to school."

The shock induced silence lingers for minutes that seem like hours. He glances up at the building again. "When I see this building, I remember the fifty-two times. This place is like a safe house and I remember being saved all those times."

And I'm worried about my children being too cold on the bus.

Elijah and I have both pleaded with God in times of peril. Whether code yellows or lions, cold buses or child sacrifices, we have both cried "Jesus!" and heaven answered. Angels received marching orders, lions turned from an easy dinner, and children were miraculously shielded from gunfire. Because we serve a God who rescues His children from the lion's mouth[29] and delivers them from evil[30]. All *we* must do is ask.

> *"I will rescue those who love me.*
> *I will protect those who trust in my name.*
> *When they call on me, I will answer;*
> *I will be with them in trouble,"*
>
> *Psalm 91:14-15.*

---

[29] 2 Timothy 4:17

[30] Matthew 6:13

When God Speaks

5

10 + 7 = 188

In God's classroom, math equations work differently. Things don't always add up the way we might expect. Pastor Elijah witnessed God's math in action when He fed, clothed, and sheltered 188 Hands of Love children for a year and half with a mere ten dollars.

Making a List, Checking it Twice

Elijah has never been a man of financial wealth. As a poor college student, he worked to pay his way through seminary training to become a pastor in the Anglican Church of Uganda. He successfully earned two bible college diplomas and a college degree. He also successfully navigated the dating world.

In 1990, Elijah met and married his wife, Ruth. It was a moment that added up to one of his life's richest blessings. "My first glance of Ruth was enough to capture me. My father and Ruth's father arranged for her to pass by a certain place where I could watch her. As she interacted with my father, I could sense her kind, meek spirit.

"Ruth has a unique spirit which captures people's favor. When you hear her speak, when you hear her preach, even just a greeting, it captures your attention. The way she greeted my father, her behavior, her mannerisms, I was captured by her. My father and I are both big talkers. That day, my dad gave Ruth the third degree, asking her many unnecessary questions. But she was patient. She was kind and continued to answer without showing disrespect."

As Elijah watched Ruth's interaction with his father from afar, he remembered a certain list he and his mother compiled just a few months earlier. A list describing Elijah's dream life partner.

*****

The water in the pot boiled as Eseza pinched the bean pods to extract the brown, kidney-shaped morsels that would become dinner. "Elijah," Eseza turned to her son, "When the time comes for you to marry, tell me the kind of woman you would like." She handed him a bean pod. Elijah squeezed it until the beans appeared. He placed them carefully into the apron of his mother's dress with the others. He studied his mother and thought hard.

"Give me some time," Elijah answered. "I need to put more thought into this." He walked into Eseza's hut where his school books were stashed. He found a blank piece of paper and a pencil and sat down to write.

The sun dipped low on the horizon as Eseza poured the cooked beans into the gourd. Movement caught her eye and she looked up. Elijah walked toward her holding a piece of paper. "I have my list, mom. These are all the things I want most in the person who will become my wife."

He held up the list and began to read. "She must be kind. She must be a woman of prayer. She needs to balance me. She mustn't be too tall or too short . . ."

When God Speaks

Better than Winning the Lottery

Elijah remembered that day with his mother as he watched the woman chat with his father. He checked off most of his mental wish list. "During the twenty-five minutes Ruth spent on her knees[31] before my father, I didn't observe every single trait I'd envisioned. But Ruth possessed *almost* everything on my list. Even the height! I especially liked her well-disciplined behavior and the way she greeted my father."

After a highly supervised courtship[32], Elijah and Ruth were married. Their life started well. Elijah graduated from seminary and became a pastor in the Anglican Church. Life was good until the end of 1991 when Christian evangelists began visiting Ruth and Elijah's home. While Elijah was busy pastoring, the "born again" believers repeatedly shared their message of salvation with Ruth. She began to listen and hear something very different from the message she was hearing in the Anglican Church[33].

In June of 1991, Ruth gave her life to Jesus Christ and began a personal relationship with Him. She stopped attending the Anglican Church—which

---

[31] Elijah and Ruth come from the Bantu people group where the formal way of greeting your elder is to approach them and sit on your knees.

[32] Ruth's conservative parents were the primary supervisors of their dates. The couple was rarely allowed to spend time alone.

[33] At this time, the Anglican Church of Uganda blended Christian doctrine with cultural rituals. Though biblical principles were taught, the true Gospel of Salvation was not preached. Instead, the main focus was on attending church and participating in religious and cultural rituals. Because of this blending, some important biblical truths were overlooked.

created quite a stir—and began praying for her husband. Ruth's prayers converged with a tenacious sixteen-year-old boy whose desire for Elijah to truly know Jesus resulted in many visits to their home. The young missionary planted many seeds.

One day, another visitor knocked on Elijah's door. The Reverend Jackson Muteba again shared the Gospel with Elijah and explained the difference between living a Christian lifestyle and having a true relationship with Jesus Christ. Something clicked inside Elijah. All the seeds, all of Ruth's prayers, and God's sovereign plan for Elijah Sebuchu imploded on his heart. On that December day, the "relationship-is-better-than-meat" pastor earnestly prayed to receive Jesus as his personal Lord and Savior. His life was never the same.

"Many people ask, 'What was your transforming moment, your life's greatest turning point?' *That* was my turning point. I believe from the bottom of my heart that when a person gives his or her life to Christ as their *personal* Lord and *personal* Savior, that is the *most* important thing. It is weightier, heavier, more precious, than a person winning a lottery of 100 billion US dollars. It is the most important thing. The most precious thing. To me my turning point as a person, as a couple, even as a family, was the time when as the head of my family, I gave my life to Jesus Christ."

But Elijah and Ruth's new salvation plus their boldness to share it with others did not equal a comfortable life. Immersed in "Christianity" that has been tainted with cultural practices such as polygamy, idol worship, and witchcraft, the Sebuchu's immediately encountered strong opposition. It began when Ruth, refusing to attend church, began challenging other church members with true salvation vs. the false Christianity they were being taught.

The ripples stirred and many people began responding to the Sebuchu's faith. This caused confusion for other members, and church officials got involved. They issued a watch on Ruth and Elijah and, eventually, sent a written warning.

*****

Elijah held the sealed envelope and took a deep breath. It was February 1992, just a few months after he had become a "born-again" Christian. He was standing in the seating area of their modest home furnished by the Anglican Church. His hands were shaky, but his heart was at rest and had been since he surrendered his life to Jesus.

He tore open the letter, unfolded it, and began reading.

Dear Pastor Sebuchu,

The board of deacons for the Anglican Church wishes to issue a warning for the sake of our church. As of the date appearing on this letter, you have exactly twenty days to renounce your new faith. If you choose to do so, you may remain an ordained pastor in the Ugandan Anglican Church and must submit a formal letter of apology to the appropriate individuals.

When God Speaks

However, if you choose to continue professing your new faith, you will no longer be welcome to serve as pastor here. You will need to submit your letter of resignation accordingly.

Please do not delay in your response. The peace and unity of our congregation is at stake.

The letter was signed by the arch deacon. Elijah reread the letter and fell to his knees. "Lord, I will not refuse You or reject my new relationship with You. But this job is the first time I have had a steady income and a secure home for my family. I will serve you faithfully, Lord. But I need you to show me what to do. Please, Lord, make a way for my family through this time."

Elijah felt a presence behind him. He turned. Ruth was standing in the entry with her eyes closed in prayer. Elijah handed her the letter and she read it slowly, carefully. He waited for her response.

She folded it quietly, placed it back in the envelope, and handed it to her husband. Her expression did not change. "This letter doesn't impress me. It's unimportant. Even if they only give us one day to make our decision, there is no decision to be made."

Elijah put his hands on Ruth's shoulders and spoke from his heart. "But Ruth, we are playing around with a very big opportunity. What's to become of us if we reject them completely? I think we need more time. We need to ask them for two years so we can organize a plan for our family."

"You mean you want to be in a pit for two years? Absolutely not!" Ruth stood with her arms crossed and stared Elijah down. "We will not be lukewarm Christians. No, never!" She protected their new faith like a lioness whose cubs were being stalked by a fierce predator.

During the first part of the twenty days, Elijah and Ruth continued to share their new faith by distributing tracts that explained the difference between being a "Christian" in name and having a true relationship with Jesus. They preached the Gospel openly. Seeing that the letter had not dissuaded the couple, the arch deacon called a district meeting with the bishop to further question Elijah.

The packed room held 273 church officials and congregants. After opening in prayer, the panel of officials questioned Elijah. His years of training to be a pastor and leader kicked in. He launched into a Holy-Spirit-inspired message, using the platform to once again share his new faith. In the audience, Ruth listened and prayed that the Lord would bring conversions and revival.

When he finished speaking, only four individuals remained. The Sebuchu's were later escorted out of their parsonage. Fortunately, Elijah had become acquainted with a born-again engineer who was working on the roads in the area. He had befriended Elijah and encouraged him to stand firm in his new faith. He arranged for Elijah and Ruth to rent an eight-by-twelve room just down the road from the Anglican Church. With great relief and gratitude, the Sebuchu's moved into their new quarters, rejoicing that God had made a way.

"That little house had holes in the floor and no toilet. We had left behind a floor with no holes and an indoor toilet. I had also left behind my identity, profession, and dignity. But we were not homeless," Elijah says.

But after one week, the owner kicked the young family out when he learned of the conflicts their faith had caused. "From that point on Ruth, our son, Meshach, and I lived on the streets."

"In Uganda, being homeless is complicated. Because of the muddy rainy season, the dusty dry season, the trash, and lack of food and fresh water, it is not like being homeless in the United States. We had a baby to care for and nowhere to live—for months. It was very painful."

The pain of homelessness is unlike anything I've heard Elijah share. It has a unique way of accosting its victims that's different than the pain of tribal violence, hunger, or jiggers.

He stares at nothing and repeats the word "painful" a dozen times, chewing on its bitter memory like a gristly piece of meat. Thick grief engulfs and nearly suffocates us.

Just when I think the hurt will swallow us both, he looks up and smiles. Joy floods the room and I can breathe again.

"But, oh my God. Thank you, Lord, for saving me!"

The Sebuchu family chose to deny themselves rather than denying Christ. God was performing holy subtraction. Though they would lose almost everything, He would give them everything needed to minister to His children. Everything including suffering.

"God was preparing me to be with the children of Hands of Love."

What Do You Want Me to Do?

Hungry and homeless, Elijah tapped into God's strength and continued preaching on the streets. Eventually, news of his street ministry spread. A Norwegian missionary, Torolf Karlsen, was looking to start a Bible college in Uganda. He heard about Elijah and offered him free tuition and rental assistance for a tiny family home. The Sebuchu's eagerly accepted Torolf's gracious offer. As he studied and preached, the young family slowly recovered from the persecution and homelessness.

After receiving his diploma from a four-year bible college, Elijah set to work on a B.A. in Theology at Alpha-Omega. As one of few highly educated pastors in the area, Elijah was in high demand as a bible college teaching assistant. Simultaneously, the young family launched into pastoring and training throughout the rural church plants. God poured forth his provision and by 1998, twenty five churches had begun. Week after week, they traveled the outlying rural areas of Kampala. Never before had Elijah seen such extreme devastation from HIV/AIDS. It wrecked him. "God used the church planting season to speak to me."

The devoted man of God had spent years preaching the Gospel and countless hours planting churches. "The pastors were thriving, new churches

When God Speaks

were springing up, and we were baptizing many people. But when I stopped to look around in the villages, I witnessed the children . . ."

Widespread flooding, disease, and hunger left hordes of abandoned children wandering the streets. Elijah came to a personal crossroads as he encountered the lifeless bodies of children lying in the bush and on trash heaps in every town. Caught between his calling to grow new churches and the ocean of immediate needs that engulfed him, Elijah begged God. *"What can I do? What do you want me to do?"*

This question marked a turning point in Elijah's life. "Throughout my life, God has spoken to me through people and events. Through the school shooting, God spoke. Through my bitter upbringing, God spoke. But at this specific time, more than any other, I needed to hear *directly* from God. I needed to know: *God, what do you want me,* Elijah, *to do?"*

298 Days

Elijah and Ruth rented a tiny room for their family of, now, six. The couple began praying and fasting. They started a dry fast (no food or water) that lasted for twenty-four hours. At the end of one day, they had not heard a single word from God. Another day and night passed. Still nothing. They extended for fifteen days, drinking only water. On the fifteenth day, they were tired, hungry and without the answer they were yearning to hear from God.

"By this time, I was thinking, *what is happening?* I felt weak, but I had heard nothing. Ruth and I concluded God desired more time with me." Elijah continued for fifteen more days, after which he was prompted to fast for another fifteen, drinking only water and eating cornmeal or bread at night. The four children wondered why their daddy never ate with them. "Your father is on a divine mission that will result into transformation of an entire nation," Ruth would tell them. Then they would pray for God to give their father strength and protect him from starvation.

The seemingly endless fast continued until Elijah reached day 150. He began to suffer from diarrhea. Rumors flew among his friends and family who were greatly concerned with his skin-and-bones condition. Most assumed he had contracted AIDS. As an extrovert who thrives off community and friendship, most days Elijah's fast felt like solitary confinement. Feeling ashamed and misunderstood, he considered throwing in the towel, rather than risk his health.

"After 150 days, I had become extremely weak and helpless. I had no fat on my body. I couldn't preach or do anything other than sleep and pray. I wanted to give up because I still hadn't heard anything from God. But I refused to lose the battle. So, I pressed on."

Elijah's already frail stature deteriorated further. He was lethargic and spent each day in a haze, drifting between prayer and rest. He'd lost count of the days, but Ruth faithfully kept track of each one. Elijah had been fasting for 298 days.

When God Speaks

Just two days shy of 300, Elijah's body needed nourishment. But more than he craved food, he hungered for a response to the fervent question he asked God forty-three weeks before.

An answer came that evening.

Don't Change the Channel

Outside the tiny room where he slept, the heavy rains turned the ground into a muddy swamp. Dreams wove through Elijah's mind in between dozing and listening to the rainfall. Suddenly, a voice said, "Wake up!" The vision that followed forever changed the course of his life.

"A figure came to where I was sleeping and woke me. I was led to a television. I sat down and began watching. On the TV screen, I began to see scenes. Each scene showed clips of suffering children. Some showed children walking naked. In another, children were drowning in floods. Interspersed between the clips of the suffering children, I began to recognize scenes from my life that depicted my own suffering as a child. Everything I saw was crystal clear."

"Then, I heard these words:

'Elijah, I want you to be hands of love to these children.'

"You might think that after so many days of longing to hear God's voice I would have been relieved. But hearing that was a very hard thing for me. It was ... complicated. I remember calling out to God saying 'NO! I am too weak!

When God Speaks

This is impossible! I have nothing—no money, no food for these children.' But the vision of the TV kept coming back, and Elijah could not change the channel.

The scenes of desperate children replayed in his mind. "God's voice rang in my ears . . . 'I want you to be hands of love.' I knew it was God's answer to my question, but I began to argue with Him. I begged Him to leave me alone. But the voice wouldn't go away." The internal struggle mounted within the spent pastor.

God had been very clear. He'd shown him the desperate plight of His children and issued a call to action. But Elijah lacked the resources to carry it out. He was a poor man with ten dollars to his name. Yet, he was also a man who had learned the hard way that nothing—not even caring for an ocean of AIDS orphans—was impossible for God.

During his spiritual tug of war, Elijah reasoned away the calling. As a father of four, he had his own family to feed. They were barely getting by now. There was no end to the number of AIDS orphans in the Kampala area. Desperate children were behind every corner and the needs didn't stop at food and clothing. Many were diseased and had serious medical conditions. Even if God did provide the basics, how would he shelter and clothe so many? What about education? The longer he questioned God's plan, the greater the obstacles seemed.

"I told God no many times but, eventually, He won me over." After days of arguing, God's answer came through clear. His words resonated so

When God Speaks

deeply that the pastor still clings to them today as he ministers to hurting children:

"When you have Me, you have everything. When you don't have Me, you have nothing!"

"That statement from God was life to me. With those words, He spoke life into the vision to love the children. I realized the greatest thing in the world is to have God. If you have God, you have all you need."

Assured and resolved to move forward, Elijah now faced the obstacle of sharing God's vision with his wife. As the family's provider, he knew what Ruth expected of him. He was convinced she would question this ambitious plan to take on an immense financial and emotional burden. But he also knew this was the first step of obedience in walking out his faith.

"When I first came out of that room, I did not tell Ruth. I was afraid . . . I had so many worries." After two weeks of keeping God's calling to himself, he finally broached the topic with his wife.

*****

Ruth knelt by a large rock and used a bowl of dingy water to scrub her husband's only pair of trousers. Standing on the threshold to their tiny room, Elijah threw a silent prayer up to the heavens before he approached his wife. A thousand canaries were caged inside his racing heart.

"I have something to tell you." The words choked out of him as he described the vision of the TV and the scenes of children. Ruth stopped scrubbing and lifted her hand, motioning for him to stop speaking. She stared intently at Elijah. Her face was stoic.

Here it comes. The knot in his stomach tightened. *What was I thinking? I cannot ask this of her. This is not the life my wife expected when she married me.*

"Elijah." The strength of her voice hushed the canaries. "I know what you are saying." Her face remained devoid of expression but her eyes locked on his with fierce intention. "God is calling us to serve the orphans. He has shared the same thing with me."

A flood of relief washed over him. The muscles he'd anxiously clenched for weeks finally relaxed. He grabbed Ruth and hugged her tightly. All at once, he knew there was nothing he and Ruth couldn't do and no child they could not reach.

"I remember the joy of that moment. I was so thankful God enabled me to endure and finish the fast. It helped me to understand my purpose on earth, my existence. Ruth's response was a major confirmation to move forward with the vision God had given us."

Prophetic Prayer

Next, the young couple discussed their plan. They visited the bank, withdrew ten dollars, and closed the account. With their life savings in their pocket, they gathered what little belongings they had and prepared their children. The family journeyed seventy-five miles on foot to Kayunga to visit Elijah's mother.

When they reached her modest rental home (a hut), Eseza was digging in the garden. After a warm greeting, Elijah shared the reason for their visit.

"I had prepared myself for a very lengthy discussion with my mother. I began describing the fast and "hands of love" vision. Once again, the reaction I got surprised me. She said 'Many years ago, I had the same vision. I saw Elijah serving the children.' Then she began to pray for us."

For forty minutes, Eseza placed her hands on Ruth and Elijah and spoke of many things God had shared through the years. She spoke of hundreds of children seated before Elijah. She described scenes with foreigners from the United States and Europe coming to Uganda. She said Elijah would meet with influential people from all over the world . . . Elijah shaking hands with powerful politicians, engaging in business meetings and speaking before international groups . . . laying hands and delivering God's healing power to AIDS victims.

God's vision and plans poured forth from Eseza as Ruth and Elijah knelt with eyes closed. When she finished she simply said, "I have given you what I have. Now go and serve God."

Empowered with words from his heavenly Father and prophecies from his earthly mother, Elijah was prepared to head for his "promised land." Their ministry would begin in the remote region of Namadhi, Mayuge district, located 185 miles from Eseza's home.

When God Speaks

Machete Man

The young couple walked four days before they reached Namadhi. Elijah was still weak physically, but a supernatural strength powered his steps. Just miles from their destination, they passed some acreage owned by a Muslim man named Bruhan Isabirye. As they approached his home, Elijah felt a strong urge to stop. The man was chopping away with a machete.

Elijah cupped his hands around his mouth. "Hello, sir!"

The man nodded a hello. "What can I do for you?"

"That is a fine tool you have," he motioned to the machete.

"Yes. I was getting hungry for some *matooke*." Bruhan gestured over to a small pile of the green bananas he'd just harvested.

"Sir, it may be a lot to ask, but I am in great need of a machete. I wonder if you would consider a loan?"

Looking intently at Elijah, the man studied his face. He looked down at the machete in his hands.

"No! I will not loan it to you," Bruhan said. "But tell me what you are going to do with it and I will give it to you."

Elijah briefly shared the vision of the children and his desire to clear the nearby land. Once again, his response was unexpected.

"What?!" Bruhan began to belly laugh. His contagious joy infected Ruth and Elijah with more laughter. This man was so overcome by the crazy

When God Speaks

audacity of what this young family was about to tackle, he could do nothing else but laugh.

Despite his apparent doubts, the man composed himself, reached down, and handed the machete to Elijah. With that selfless gesture, Bruhan became the very first Hands of Love in-kind donor.

When Elijah remembers Bruhan, their unlikely meeting, and the divine provision of the machete, he shakes his head in amazement. "For God to begin work, He doesn't have to wait for the resources. It's important for anyone called by God to learn this truth. If God has given you the vision, move on with it! *First* you move, then the resources will find you on the way. The truth is, where there is a vision, there is a *pro*vision!"

Seven Mud Huts

With little more than Bruhan's machete in hand, Ruth, Elijah, and their four small children reached their bush-covered destination after a tiring four-day walk. The promised land to which God had directed them was the land willed to Elijah by his grandfather, the former Kasimba clan chief.

When God Speaks

Ruth and Elijah were utterly exhausted. A rickety mud hut left over from the land's previous owner was a welcome place for them to sleep. With their last shred of energy, they spread palm branches on the mud floor and collapsed. For the next two weeks, they cleared a large expanse of trees and jungle-like overgrowth using the only tools they had: their bare hands and the machete.

Next, they set out to construct circular, mud and wattle huts with cone-shaped, palm branch roofs using mud, sticks, and plants. It was exhausting work and their fuel consisted of only jackfruit, pawpaws, and anything else the bush plants produced.

After eleven days, children started appearing out of nowhere. As Ruth gathered firewood or walked to draw water, she would catch movement behind her. While out one day, she turned to see two curious eyes peering out from behind a mango tree. One by one, they came until there were 188 children.

For a family of six to survive in the African bush with barely any food, no medical care, and no clean water or proper shelter would be remarkable. But the survival of two adults with 192 children amidst these conditions was miraculous.

One of the original wattle huts constructed by Elijah and Ruth

"Not just once a day, but *many* times a day, our lives were threatened. These hungry, vulnerable children were relying on us to keep them alive. To this day, I'm still amazed and thankful to God that we survived those first weeks."

From hordes of mosquitoes to deadly disease, today Elijah cannot remember all of the myriad obstacles they overcame. The sleeping conditions were difficult, the insects relentless, but hunger was by far their greatest enemy.

"The first year, the biggest challenge for me was food supply. It was painful watching so many children go hungry. We had no clothes to give them, no means to educate them, no money to pay for staff . . . no nothing! Resources were non-existent."

"We prayed often and God provided—miraculously provided. Sometimes complete strangers who'd heard of our work would bring us fruit and leftover food. We drank water harvested from banana leaves when it rained. A friend sold his charcoal and bought a thin mattress for the tiny children to sleep on. We prayed and we were creative." Ruth and Elijah walked back to their church in Kampala and gathered old bed sheets. They used the worn-out sheets to "clothe" as many children as possible. But the time came when clothing was not the first priority.

"We were forced to make hard choices. Even if the children grew up naked, scraping together enough money to buy books and pay teachers was far more important. Poverty results not from lack of clothing, but lack of education. So, we placed a high priority on education," Elijah said.

The work was not only hard, there were endless needs and unanticipated complications. "Some of the children could not speak. Unfortunately, that meant they couldn't tell us their name. One would say, 'My name is Jared.' The next day he'd say, 'I'm Timothy.' One of our kids named Isaac has changed his name seven times! First he said Esau, but eventually he became Isaac."

Because the state required all students to have birth certificates to be eligible for the critical national exam, full names and birthdates were essential. Unless the children were old enough to know their birthdays, Elijah and Ruth had no way to obtain this information. So they simply made them up.

"I can remember one of many forms I completed," Elijah says. "I was just making up dates for the forms. I was so exhausted, I wrote October 36 as the child's birth date!"

As time marched on, it was clear the ten dollars God had stretched would only stretch so far. If they wanted to keep caring for children, they would need more resources. It was time to widen the playing field.

Virtual Friendship = Substantial Resources

A few years before the ministry's inception, Elijah had received computer training from a friend. When the friend learned of Elijah and Ruth's orphan ministry, he proposed a new way to address the problem of resources. Elijah put his new skills to practice, using the Internet to search for available funds. He created an e-mail address for Hands of Love and notified international missions organizations about the ministry.

When God Speaks

On the other side of the globe, in Germany, a man named Dittmar Knollenborg was skimming his e-mail inbox. His finger hit the delete key again and again as he scrolled through junk mail. Just as he was about to delete a newsletter sent by Open Heaven Digest, he hesitated, then reconsidered and opened it. He scrolled down and read about a couple caring for 188 children in rural Uganda. Dittmar was intrigued and quickly composed an e-mail. The subject line read: "I come or you come."

Elijah read the e-mail suggesting he visit Germany. But he quickly replied, "Man, you won't believe my stories if I come to Germany. You must come and see this with your own eyes!" Elijah followed up by mailing a formal letter of invitation, and two weeks later, Hands of Love received its first Western missionary.

Dittmar visited nineteen of Elijah's church plants then traveled to remote Namadhi. He spent several weeks serving and provided the impoverished orphans with a generous supply of food. It was the first time in eight months the children had consistent nourishment. Before that, the meager food supply meant they typically went a day or sometimes longer between meals.

"The children would finish their rice and begin eating the paper plate. Dittmar was overwhelmed and deeply moved by what he saw," Elijah says. Never before had the civilized Westerner seen such hunger. Never again would he use the phrase, "I'm starving," regardless of how hungry he was. He had seen what starving truly looked like.

When it was time for Dittmar's departure, he took Elijah by the hand and escorted him to the German Embassy where he waded through Ugandan bureaucracy, completed the necessary paperwork and secured a VISA for Elijah. Back in Germany, Christel Hetzer, a hand extending friend of Dittmar's, worked around the clock to raise funds for Elijah's airfare.

Dittmar's visit was a game changer for the children of Hands of Love. God had performed another unlikely addition problem:

1 German missionary + 1 Ugandan pastor = Globalization of HOL

During Elijah's visit to Germany, six children received sponsors. Among them were John and Linda Gray who would later found Hands of Love UK. Two of the group's supporters, Barrie and Eileen Jones connected Elijah with their American daughter Anna Latshaw. In 2008, Anna founded Hands of Love USA in Marietta, GA. One year later, Hands of Love USA began building the second orphanage and school in Kabaga-Kampala, Uganda.

Eseza's prophetic prayers were coming to pass. Elijah was about to set foot on his first airplane to meet with groups of international leaders and speak before them. The group of children she dreamed of was growing and would eventually reach 2,600. And it all started with ten dollars and a machete.

That's miraculous multiplication.

When God Speaks

Less is More

Elijah saw the ravages of starvation and starved himself until he heard God speak. His spiritual hunger superseded his physical hunger.

When God chose Elijah, perhaps it was because the hungry, homeless children of Uganda needed God more than they needed food. I suppose that's why Elijah's lack of resources was no problem for God. There would have been a small wrinkle in the plan, though, if Elijah had lacked God or the desire for God. He opened a hand by asking "what can I do," and the ripple effect has made all the difference. And it's still making all the difference today.

When you want to follow God more than you want food or luxuries, you do crazy stuff like empty your bank account and walk seventy-five miles to clear acres of jungle by hand. And it doesn't have to be a 300-day fast. God looks at the heart, not the size of the sacrifice.

*****

Jay is a friend with a huge heart. He always has a smile and a hug for me. Jay's a great hugger. But Jay's hugs are not what I like most about him. He is a super successful attorney. But that's not what I admire most about him either. Jay has the gift of generosity, and because he loves Jesus, he does crazy stuff. He's a crazy, hand-extending kind of guy. I love that about him.

When God Speaks

One day he invited me for coffee and said he had something to tell me. Pastor Elijah and Jay had met briefly at our church the day before. Over Chick-fil-A coffee, Jay shared how he really liked Elijah and the Hands of Love story. After some more small talk, Jay reached into his brief case and pulled out a Rolex watch.

I like nice things but I'm not so much a fancy jewelry kind of girl. So, at first, I didn't recognize the box. But Jay began to share with me that he'd bought the watch years ago when he was a young, jet-setting attorney in Washington DC. An in-the-know friend advised him to "look the look."

Generous Jay struggled with the extravagant purchase but chose to buy the watch on one condition. If, at any time, God wanted him to give the watch away, he'd do it. The day Jay shook Elijah's hand, God gave him the "go" sign. It was time for the Rolex to make its way to Atlanta, where the Hands of Love folks could sell it to pay education fees for hundreds of high school kids.

Generous Jay understands that in God's upside-down kingdom economy, less is more. I like how actor and activist Ed Begley, Jr. says it:

"We, who have so much, must do more to help those in need. And, most of all, we must live simply, so that others may simply live." What does living simply look like practically? That is up to you and God. But here are some ideas for starters:

- Shop at Goodwill or your local thrift store. Hunt for new items—I'm always surprised at how many still have the tag on.

Whatever you saved off the ticketed price, set aside for the least of these.

- If you're a coffee addict, put a plastic box in your car or keep a running tab on your smart phone. Brew coffee at home. When you drive by your favorite coffee joint on the way to work put three dollars in the box or on your savings tally. At the end of the month, give it away. If you did this just four days of every week, in one month you'd have saved more than enough to sponsor a Hands of Love child!
- Give up soft drinks at fast food restaurants. Order water instead and donate a buck or two for every drink you didn't consume.
- Do you shop at Amazon? Go to Smile.Amazon.com and register to support Hands of Love Foundation Inc. (Marietta GA). Amazon will automatically donate .5% of every purchase. This costs you nothing.
- $5.00 bill challenge. Every time you receive a $5.00 bill, put it in a jar. At the end of the year empty your jar and donate the money to Hands of Love.
- Round-up your spare change. Connect your credit/debit card to the Hands of Love Donor account. Your card purchases will round-up to the next dollar as change. Your 'Round-up' change accumulates and is donated to Hands of Love each month (https://handsofloveusa.org/round-up-how-it-works/).

When God Speaks

As a Christian raised in the United Methodist Church, I've always admired John Wesley. Recently I learned something that made me love the guy even more. In the late 1700s, the government taxed anyone who owned anything made of silver. The more you had, the more you paid. In 1776, the commissioners accused Wesley of failure to declare silver, therefore avoiding the tax. Wesley responded: "I have two silver spoons at London and two at Bristol. This is all the silver I own at present, and I shall not buy any more while so many around me want bread."

Generous Jay and John Wesley understand the meaning of living simply so others might simply live. Like Elijah, they act on their belief that when you have God, you have everything. And when they hear the "I'm starving" cries of children (who really are starving) they extend a hand and make a change.

What hand will you extend to start living more simply?

6

Oasis of Joy in a Desert of Despair

Our car is greeted by a sea of lush, green palms fanning back and forth in joyful homage. We have just motored through the front gate at Hands of Love's Namadhi orphanage. The children chant their greeting in cheerful triplets: "*Wel-o-come! Wel-o-come!*" They flash smiles as wide as nearby Lake Victoria.

Dan, Elijah, and I step out of the car. Hordes of five- to twelve-year-olds, buzzing with energy, swarm us. With high fives at the ready, they wait, open-palmed, hoping to grasp ours, if only for a moment. We are *wazungu* "royalty," and our "red carpet" is the front drive in Namadhi[34]. Our "paparazzi" is Cyrus Muwonge, the school's diligent videographer. Our arms are laden with bouquets of local flowers. Hand-crafted signs advertise what our over-the-top reception has made obvious: We certainly are most welcome to Hands of Love.

Soon after, we are whisked away to the headmaster's office for a short introduction. Headmaster Joseph eagerly greets us, gesturing toward two straight-backed wooden chairs. His hospitality and energetic charm more than make up for what his office lacks in modern comforts. No running water,

---

[34] Namadhi is located approximately 185 miles northeast of Kampala. By car, the journey takes approximately four hours due to poor road conditions.

coffeemakers, or laptops here. On the floor next to Joseph's desk, a car battery charges a collection of cell phones. Although the school's remote location offers no infrastructure for phone cables, cell tower signals provide critical communication to the team of thirty-nine who serve 1,300 plus children. Just outside, a donated solar panel soaks up the intense rays of the equatorial sun. In turn, the car battery is charged—in Uganda, there's more than one way to skin a cat, and charge a phone.

Neatly scripted on canary-yellow poster board that hangs on the main wall, the school vision beckons us:

To Educate and Empower

National and International Christian Leaders

Who Will Cause Transformation?

Elijah and his staff serve tirelessly to realize this goal and convince the children of its truth. Inspired by this vision, the key leaders don't simply buy into transformation, many of them have lived through it themselves. Born into the very same poverty as the children they serve, they too have overcome and been "raised from the dust."

Take Primary School Headmaster Joseph, who oversees twenty-one staff and thirteen hundred students. Dozens of candidates vied alongside Joseph for his position. What made him an outstanding candidate wasn't an impressive degree, years of experience, or prestigious schooling. Joseph's desire to serve the children set him apart.

Elijah seeks men and women who will allow God's vision to pulsate through every decision, lesson, and conversation. He lives by the leadership principle that "the greatest among us are those who are willing to be servants."[35]

Seated in the principal's office, Elijah, my husband, and I enjoy a home-cooked lunch. Secondary (Middle) School Headmistress and Hands of Love Supervisor, Namadhi, Annet, awoke early to prepare our delicious meal. On her floor, a plastic banner, which once announced a church event, now doubles as carpet. The recycled sign and other clues point out what's missing and which material resource is needed. Bare floors = no carpeting. Oil lanterns = no lights. Kids climbing trees and eating with their hands = no playground equipment or utensils. But for each instance of lack, there are a dozen lessons of hope:

- Eager hands pump plentiful, clean drinking water from a donated well.

---

[35] Matthew 23:11

When God Speaks

- Strong legs run through a school yard where donated playground balls bounce.

- Heaping plates of rice, meat, and beans are doled out to hungry bellies.

When God Speaks

It doesn't take long to see that hope lives here—hope that's made possible by servant leaders and generous donors who wrote checks faster than you can say "There are hungry kids in Uganda." Hope rises amidst a circle of fifty teenagers who raise joyful voices and hands in worship. They sway and sing praises to the One who provided them with a home, an education, and many, many new friends. The hope here is unmistakable. It's no wonder the "gate-watchers" want in.

The "Gate-Watchers"

A shoddy fence stands about thirty yards away from the circle of praising youth. It separates the Hands of Love children from the surrounding villages. In these rural parts, lack runs rampant and hope is yet to surface. On the other side of the fence, poverty chokes out education, usurping a child's learning time for hours in the rice fields. It steals long division lessons and school yard soccer scrimmages from ten-year-olds.

This morning, before our arrival at the Hands of Love gates, Stephen drove us through the scrubby Mayuge region. We sat comfortably in our air-conditioned car while Pastor Elijah introduced us to village after village of poverty's victims. We watched nine-year-olds thresh rice, pounding the chaff onto stones till their hands blistered.

We saw children of six years walking miles for water, babies strapped on their backs. Babies carrying babies. We saw young boys digging holes and planting cassava and toddlers whose legs wobbled under the weight of the bricks they carried. Poverty's converts are the street children we passed whose hunger pangs drive them to steal bananas from a roadside grove and scavenge scraps from trash cans.

Most Hands of Love children formerly wandered "from nowhere to nowhere," Elijah explains. Many were abandoned when their parents could no longer afford food and clothing. The streets became home. Random verandas or banana trees provided temporary shelter. Unfortunately, it is not uncommon for staff to find crowds of such wanderers lined up outside the orphanage after westerners visit. The homeless "gate-watchers" assume that once wealthy *wazungu* leave, there will be money left behind, allowing Hands of Love to take in more kids. With hearts aching, staff members must refuse those children chanting, "Let us in!"

The day after our visit to the Namadhi location, more than one hundred fifty kids gathered, clamoring to enter. They were turned away. The words drift back, echoing inside me: "Each day, the staff at Hands of Love refuse, on average, *eighty children*."

When God Speaks

Sponsored vs. Unsponsored

Inside the gates, uniformed children scurry to classrooms, and cooks prepare lunch. Foreign spices pepper our western noses, wafting from enormous vats of beef, posho, rice and beans. Uniforms and meals are made possible by sponsors who contribute fifty dollars per month. Unsponsored children wear hand-me-downs and eat only posho with an occasional meal of meat or beans.

A self-evident truth emerges as we interact with the two classes of children: *even the unsponsored children are blessed.* They are not wanderers, trash-pickers, or beggars. They receive the same education, love, and security as the sponsored children.

The unbalanced arrangement begs the question of jealousy. But Elijah explains that from the moment a child comes to Hands of Love, they are taught to celebrate with those who receive the blessing.

"An American missionary once visited and made a connection with some homeless children in a nearby village. She phoned her home church to secure new sponsors. All of sudden I showed up at the orphanage with ten new children. I came to Hands of Love and told the kids awaiting sponsors what was happening. What did those children do? The unsponsored children began celebrating! They were not bitter. They didn't say 'No! It's not their turn.[36]' No, they did not! They began *celebrating*. Because we always pray more children

---

[36] The order in which children receive sponsors is typically determined by case workers and other staff based on the level of greatest need.

will get sponsors, and when I brought new children in, they saw God answers their prayers."

Another answer to prayer for unsponsored children is the provision of foster homes. Approximately eight hundred children have been placed in such homes located near both Hands of Love schools. Families are carefully scrutinized and must pass through a system of security checks before they are approved as a host home. This arrangement allows the orphanage to care for and educate fostered children on site even when they lack the physical resources to provide adequate shelter. The added benefit of belonging and the sense of family do wonders for their emotional well-being.

Following the Leader

As we move among these powerful young leaders-in-the-making, we, too, follow the leader. Pastor Elijah shakes hands, bumps fists, and embraces his children. He knows each of their names and every life story. He kneels down to pray with one who is ill, lays hands and asks God to restore her. The atmosphere around us seems to shift as he prays. Darkness becomes light.

Fourteen-year-old Robert walks confidently toward us. He and the pastor embrace. "Hello, Robert, mighty man of God!" Elijah's deep voice bellows. "This one wants to be a doctor," he says as he squeezes Roberts shoulder. Just as a conscientious father would, he reminds each student to focus. "Isaac, how are your studies? . . . Are you working very hard, Victoria?"

When God Speaks

Victoria and Isaac are two of the original 188 "bush orphans." They lived in the seven mud huts with Pastors Elijah and Ruth ten years ago. Today these students study rigorously and will soon graduate with the rest of the first class at Hands of Love.

The student dormitories are our next stop. The rudimentary brick building sleeps two hundred fifty kids in neat rows of bunk beds and approximately one hundred fifty more on the cement floor. All sponsored children receive a bed, mattress, sheets, and blankets. One student's tidy bed is personalized with a handkerchief hung from the bunk above. Its magic-markered message reminds us, and the one who sleeps under it each night, that "God Is Good All the Time."

Papyrus mats on the floor between the bunk beds provide unsponsored children with a safe and dry—albeit hard—place to get their rest tonight. Not exactly the Ritz Carlton. But ask a child who sleeps here, even on the mats, about their preference? They would choose the floor here over where they came from any day of the week. While the geography of where they came from might vary by village name, conditions are usually similar.

Hugs and Belonging

For any child, security is critical. For Uganda's orphans, it is beyond rare. Most of these wandering children are ravaged by fear before arriving at Hands of Love. Wild animals, kidnappers, cannibals, and those who wish to engage in child sacrifice are just a few of their worst enemies.

Child sacrifice? Learning how lack of food impacts these children has been hard to swallow. Understanding how they wander from "nowhere to nowhere" is disturbing. But we were blindsided by the harsh reality that child sacrifice is a rampant problem here.

"In Kampala alone, an average of seventeen children are *known* to be sacrificed every day. Only fifteen percent of the people of Uganda live in Kampala. That means hundreds of unreported cases of child sacrifice are likely happening elsewhere. Many cases are known, but, due to fear of repercussions by corrupt law enforcement, people are afraid to report them," Elijah explains.

According to a BBC News report, "human sacrifice is on the increase in Uganda. The crime is directly linked to rising levels of development and prosperity, and an increasing belief that witchcraft can help people get rich quickly."[37]

"There are lots of false beliefs," Elijah says. "Some people who practice polygamy believe that by sacrificing their first wife or first-born child, they can consult demon gods for wealth. The gods will tell you to 'sacrifice twelve children and bring us the heads,' or 'only children with a gap between their front teeth,' or 'children that are always smiling.' The more desperate people are, the more willingly they buy into such myths."

Uganda's desperation caused by abject poverty has also fueled widespread kidnapping. Kidnapped children are sacrificed or taken hostage.

---

[37] Source: http://news.bbc.co.uk/2/hi/8441813.stm

"Kidnappers will often ask up to $25,000 US dollars to ransom a child," Elijah says. High-profile Ugandans are often targets for these crimes, but no child in Kampala is off limits. Even poor children are at risk.

Because of the staggering danger that threatens Kampala's children, Elijah and his staff relish the opportunity to provide security and a sense of belonging.

"One of my great privileges is to give children hugs, because I missed that growing up," Elijah says. "I don't remember spending any time—even one full hour—with my father, except on my wedding day. That day, I received my first hug from my father. I will never forget this mission: to always give hugs to the children."

A national figure, Pastor Elijah's receives around 5,000 public speaking invitations per year. But he would rather be seated on the grass surrounded by "his children" than speaking before the Ugandan Parliament. "All my life, the one thing that consumes me above any other ministry is to love and serve the children.

"Whenever I return after taking major international trips, my staff want me to schedule meetings at the office. But my priorities are with the children. More than anything, I love to sit down on the grass and just visit with them. They inspire me. These children are like my own kids—I've been with them for so long."

School Administrator Samuel agrees. He thrives on the joy he gets from serving the orphans. "If I'm tired or fatigued, when the children come to me, there is no more fatigue. That is why I serve here full-time. They also feel so happy when they see me. It has changed my life. I feel like this is my green pasture. This is where I belong."

How many kids do you have?

A sense of belonging is precisely what Hands of Love aims to offer abused, orphaned, and neglected children. Admittedly, when Dan and I began sponsoring Samuel, it seemed a pathetic substitute for a real family. Elijah insisted our monthly gift would make a big difference. But we wondered, "Could fifty dollars a month truly change a child who lives several thousand miles away?"

Two days prior to our grand Hands of Love welcome, our plane touched down at Entebbe International Airport in Uganda, just minutes before midnight. As expected, we were warmly greeted by Pastor Elijah's key missionary liaisons. We were unprepared, however, for the huge smile and warm embrace of our eight-year-old sponsored son Samuel, who stayed up *way* past his normal bed time to greet us!

Our sponsor relationship began in 2011, a long-distance bond formed through photos, cards, and letters. But the night we arrived in Africa, we were blown away by how Samuel behaved toward us—two American strangers. He immediately held our hands and began calling us "mommy and daddy." He asked questions about his "brother and sister" back in Charleston. He couldn't get enough time with "his parents."

When God Speaks

*****

Dan and I sit next to Samuel at lunch the next day. We are hanging out around a school table in Principal Sarah's office, making small talk with the school staff. "How many children do you have?" someone asked.

"Two," Dan says. "We have a daughter who is fifteen and a younger son who's thirteen."

"No!" insists a small voice beside Dan. Samuel holds up three fingers. "Three!" A bashful grin creeps across his face.

Dan laughs and give his second son a huge high five. "You are right! I stand corrected. We have three children. Two in the United States and one here, in Uganda."

Samuel's grin grows wider and my heart, like the Grinch who stole Christmas, grows *three sizes as I watch him high-five his dad.*

"Samuel will think of you as his family," our sponsor coordinator had stated in the detailed e-mail explaining our support agreement. "Oh, how

Samuel 2014   Samuel 2019

sweet," we thought. But our time with Samuel cements the truth that, in the heart and mind of a Hands of Love child, sponsorship means *belonging*. Sponsorship offers way more than a pleasant notion to lift an orphan's spirits. It gives each child a feeling of significance and a true sense of belonging. Samuel says it best: "The day I was told of my sponsorship was the best, most important day of my life."

Hands of Love Sponsorship Coordinator, Solomy echoes this truth. "When a child gets sponsored, he becomes completely happy. You see it changing their outlook. Before sponsorship, some struggle to maintain hope.

When God Speaks

But when they get a sponsor, their life totally changes. They become more open, more talkative. They begin praying with friends. It changes everything for them.

"When they first arrive here, they are not sure they will be able to stay," Solomy continues. Orphaned children are used to being relocated from a distant relative's house to a foster home. Nomadic backgrounds cause uncertainty and fear. "Sponsorship is the first proof that this truly is their home. It secures their future. They come in hopeless, but after receiving a sponsor and education, they begin believing in a bright future that offers great hope."

Tomorrow's Leaders

Touring the grounds of the school, we come face to face with the transformed: students who are tomorrow's leaders. These leaders will transform their nation, refusing to heed poverty's lies

"When we get sponsors, we get new parents who make us forget our troubles and background, which was very bad," says Mary, a fourteen-year-old student at Hands of Love Namadhi. "I receive many things from my sponsors, but what is most important is that I've got parents who love me. I'm also proud of my education." Mary is working diligently and aspires to become a judge, who will one day rule the courtroom with love, compassion, and fairness.

It is easy to envision a secure future for fifteen-year-old Jessica. "I have the best education in the whole nation," she says with fierce confidence. "Because of what I'm learning here, I will be able to earn a good living and have a good future." Thanks to her top-notch education, Jessica boldly envisions a future for herself as a surgeon.

Casting vision to the children of Uganda is in Pastor Elijah's blood. He uses every opportunity to empower and firmly believes that no child is too young, too poor, or too ignorant to make a difference.

"Fifty percent of people in Uganda are children under fifteen years. The biggest part of our population is children. *You* have great potential to change this nation," he says. The children at Hands of Love have gathered for an assembly. They lean in, listening intently as he speaks a message of hope. "In the midst of you here, I see the president of Uganda. I see great pastors, politicians, pilots, teachers, and parents.

"The person who will change this country is not the president. Not the prime minister. Elijah Sebuchu will not change this nation. The teachers will not change the nation. It is *you* who will change this nation," he tells the students.

I am NOT an orphan!

On the "must-see-TV" list of any Hands of Love tour is a beloved ritual familiar to every child. It is the pinnacle of Elijah's pep talks—a tradition that never grows old.

When God Speaks

The pastor stands before rows and rows of children seated on the concrete floor of a large classroom. Their energized "daddy" wears a gigantic smile and waits patiently for the crowd to settle. Excited chatter eases to a hush as the familiar chant begins. Elijah feeds the children words of life. They eat them up.

Elijah feeding 'words of life' to high school students

"Somebody say, I am not poor . . ." He smiles and juts out arms to either side, arms that seem to stretch a mile wide.

The children echo: "I am not poor!"

"I am rich . . .
　　　　　I am rich!

When God Speaks

I am NOT an orphan . . .
        I am NOT an orphan!

I have my Father . . .
        I have my Father!

My Father is in Heaven . . .
        My Father is in Heaven!

He has good plans for me . . .
        He has good plans for me!

In the name of Jesus . . .
        In the name of Jesus!

I am going to transform Uganda . . .
        I am going to transform Uganda!

Hallelujah!
        Hallelujah!

I will never forget the force of 1,300 powerful, young voices chanting out hope at the top of their lungs. Their words soar. Joy reverberates off the mud walls leaving us reeling. Even *we* are changed. With each declaration, we watch

When God Speaks

as the truth roots deeper into their hearts and minds. We listen and believe it in our core.

Yes, these children *are* rich. And yes, they *will* change Uganda.

But they can't do it alone . . .

When God Speaks

God Has these Children

I approach a praise circle formed by some students under the massive banyan tree. Their vocal harmonies flood the shaded corner of the school yard. Their raw and potent worship moves me. In this moment, Richard Evans' words ring true: "It is often in the darkest skies that we see the brightest stars."

The "stars" at Hands of Love shine even more brightly against Uganda's dark backdrop of hopelessness and poverty. They don't grumble about the lack, but instead hold fast to hope, work hard at their studies, and press on to become effective Christian leaders. Their stark circumstances taunt "you'll never make it!" With bold faith, they respond, "oh yes we will!"

The contrast is stunning, especially at the Namadhi orphanage. It's an unlikely recipe for success: 1,300 orphans (many ill), a smattering of teachers (most unsalaried), two headmasters, one barely operable clinic, a few dirt-floored buildings, scarce food, and a piece of yellow posterboard.

But when you join God in His work, practical outcomes are blown away by the miraculous. All things are possible. Or, as Pastor Elijah often says, "When you have God, you have everything."

When God Speaks

Hands of Love children believe *If God did it for Pastor Elijah, why wouldn't He do it for me?* They are served helpings of hope that sustain their hearts far more effectively than the rice that fills their empty bellies.

"Shining stars" rarely start out with audacious faith, but with a mustard seed of faith. When you are neck deep in an ocean of suffering, who wouldn't be tempted to think there's no way I'll make a difference? But those who extend their hands refuse to focus on what they don't have or cannot do. Instead they focus on God and what He will do through their mustard seed. As we ride along a Kampala city street, Elijah's hands of love lessons continue.

"I am privileged to be just one part of God's big plan. I did not find God, He found me! I am not the Alpha. God's ministry did not start with me, it started with Him. God's ministry won't end with me. He is the Omega. He will not mention Elijah at the start. He will not mention Elijah at the end.

"Every day," he continues, "my mind is troubled by the eighty kids who are turned away. If unlimited resources were available, I could build homes for children all over Uganda. Some of these children come alone, soaked from the rain, others come with bleeding wounds, rashes, swollen tummies . . . I look at them and say *God, I know what they have gone through*. I have lived on the streets. I know it is very painful. Very, *very* painful."

But knowing that "God has these children," helps Elijah and others maintain perspective. Often when Elijah shares about his work, people may respond with something like, "I wish I could help Hands of Love, but I am sponsoring five children with World Vision."

When God Speaks

"I hug them and say, 'Thank you! You are saving five lives!' Now, I could think, 'But what about the children at Hands of Love? But then I'm reminded that I did not create those children! My part is to do *my* part, speak *my* part, work *my* part, and share with others the opportunity of serving the children. I leave the rest to God. It takes the pressure off."

If Elijah had not asked "what's my part?" 2,600 children would either be dead or wandering the streets of Uganda. Have you considered whom God might rescue if you were to ask Him the same question?

Look around you—right where you live—and open your hand. "If there is a poor man with you, one of your brothers, in any of your towns in your land which the Lord your God is giving you, you shall not harden your heart, nor close your hand from your poor brother," Deuteronomy 15:7.

Your "land" may look entirely different from Elijah's. Doing your part will require your unique gifts and passions and will bless another in a way no other can. Let God take the pressure off. Simply ask God "what's my part?" Open your hand.

The rest is up to God.

7

To Lead is to Serve

It's no accident that Elijah believes in the power of teamwork. Raised by a mom who taught him to value relationship above food, he has an organic desire to build and maintain strong networks. It's part of who he is. With a current staff of over 300, he lives and breathes the ancient African proverb: *If you want to go fast, go alone. If you want to go far, go together.*

As a type-A visionary, Elijah has been tempted to pull rank and use his credentials and clout to advance his ministry. But with God's help, the natural-born leader matured into one who instead might be found washing his principal's feet, wiping a child's drippy nose, or picking up trash.

"He has a father's heart." Soft-spoken Samuel is the School Administrator in Hands of Love's Namadhi orphanage. "The way he takes care of the young children and takes care of us—he is a servant of God."

Samuel describes the ripple effect of Elijah's servant's heart. "He loves the staff and the children so much. He is a man who encourages. Who has encouraged me in many, many ways. If he sees you are a little weak, he comes and says, 'No, you are powerful! You are great. He offers encouraging words and he builds us up. He walks and talks with the staff. He visits and prays with the children. As I watch him serve, God enables me to have that heart also."

Elijah, Samuel, and the other Hands of Love staff are governed by a powerful principle: *servant leadership*. It is so tightly woven into the tapestry of the ministry, you might think Elijah has always led this way. But he learned from experience that being a leader is not the same as being a boss.

No Bosses Allowed

"I've tried being a boss," Elijah says. "When I was earning my student degree, I was elected student leader of 148 students. I tried being a boss to them. I even changed my voice to make myself sound boss-like. But I realized that you will fail miserably when you are a boss, but with servanthood, you will see big progress—big breakthroughs."

Elijah sees the deficit of servants as a worldwide epidemic. "Organizations and governments that are in crisis are often afflicted with this same problem. They are craving servants. I studied the history of Uganda. One reason our nation has struggled is because of the politicians, parents, and leaders who served *themselves*."

"When I began my life as a pastor, I saw many congregations failing and members grumbling because the church leaders were bosses. I saw bishops and archbishops being bosses over God's people. Today, marriages are in crisis because men want to be bosses over their wives and children. Institutions are in disarray because the higher a person rises within the organization, the more prideful that person becomes in their spirit. What's lacking? *Servants*."

When God Speaks

"The moment I switched to this type of leadership . . . *wow*! I realized it was contagious. My staff looked up to me as their leader but then they watched me being a servant. Once our ministry was serving around the city, helping to beautify the neighborhoods near the Hands of Love Kabaga-Kampala orphanage. As I picked up trash, I noticed a look of shock on people's faces. They couldn't believe that Pastor Elijah, founder of Hands of Love, was collecting trash. All the pastors and leaders who came, they were all rolling up their sleeves like the others.

"Every morning, one of my prayers is for servants: that fathers and mothers would be servants to their children, politicians would be servants to the people. When you focus on giving, and helping people get what they want, you eventually get what *you* want. The more you serve, the more God will lift you up. That is not only biblical but practical. I've seen it work.

"Servanthood stands on its own merits when put into practice, but it is also clearly stated in scripture. Jesus modeled servant leadership. It's why He succeeded 100 percent."

It's Not a Job. It's a Calling.

Servanthood is not a new concept for Christians. The word "servant" is part of our vernacular in American churches. We talk about having a servant's heart, serving on a mission team, serving in the nursery or as an usher. We are all about serving, which is a great thing. The question is, why do we serve? Is the motive an expression of worship and gratitude to our Heavenly Father from His child? Or are we trying to prove something, cancel a debt, or seek approval?

My Ugandan brothers and sisters serving at Hands of Love are driven by a divine motivation. They are not out to prove anything. Instead, their service is fueled by the heavenly satisfaction of joining God in His work. That satisfaction provides the supernatural energy needed to meet an exhausting host of needs. And their rewards are eternal.

"It's not a job . . . it's a calling," says Annet, principal & Hands of Love supervisor, who lives and serves at Hands of Love's Secondary (Middle) School. In 2009, Annet was hired from hundreds of applicants to join Elijah's team at the rural Namadhi orphanage as a full-time staff member with no pay. With countless unmet needs among the children, resources were directed towards higher priorities than staff salaries. Annet applied her administrative and teaching gifts and the students began to excel. In 2011, the once obscure school began drawing national media attention for its academics.

A couple of years later, Annet's summa cum laude degree earned her another job offer. The $3,500 employment package included an attractive monthly salary, housing, and other privileges. She received intense pressure from her parents to accept the new job.

But Annet's deep conviction in her calling compelled her to decline the offer. Instead of embracing the comforts of more money and prestige, Annet

When God Speaks

made the choice to continue living on 100 dollars per month[38] in dusty, primitive surroundings.

"I am convinced in my heart that I'm meant to be here. However difficult the conditions may be, I was born to serve these children," she says.

Servants like Annet don't need a corner office, electricity, or even indoor plumbing. When you serve God, challenges become opportunities. Teaching computer skills to middle school children without computers might deter other teachers. For Annet, this is not a problem, but an opportunity to trust God. She exudes faith and confidence, not pompously, but in a nothing's-gonna-bring-me-down approach. When asked to describe her job's greatest challenge, a puzzled expression flashes across her brow.

"I don't have 'greatest challenges' because I came here knowing that I would be serving the children. I don't call them challenges. They are just daily happenings. With God and the help of the other staff, I am equipped to handle these."

Jesus said, "If you cling to your life, you will lose it; but if you give up your life for me, you will find it.[39]" Annet, Samuel, and Elijah have found their lives. They have laid down what the world calls success and let God and His children redefine it. They find success in the quiet confidence of a child who

---

[38] Annet's monthly salary is generously provided by an American sponsor.

[39] Matthew 10:39

just scored her first 100 in math. And who knows? That child may one day become a teacher, or doctor, or parent who follows their lead and choose to serve, rather than be served.

Building a Family

In a nation where an entire generation has been exterminated by HIV/AIDS, many have grown up without families, especially in the last twenty-five years. Fortunately for Uganda, God is still in the business of seeking out families for those without.

As their pastor and stand-in father, Elijah instills a sense of family into his staff. "The big thing is not money or stature. The big thing is family— belonging. In the book of Genesis, God said it is not good for man to be alone. We read that and we often think about marriage. But the bigger picture is that it's not good for any person to be alone. We need family— we need to belong.

"God has chosen me to be a father to the fatherless; to treasure people and love them as family. I have always told the children that they are not orphans, that they have a father and a family."

Among both the children and staff, Pastor Elijah has earned the term of endearment, "Papa." It's not uncommon to see him sharing hugs, high fives and laughter with his team. "That keeps us together. It is powerful. We are one tribe: the tribe of Jesus Christ. Serving together, treating one another as family—it's helping to heal many people's wounds. Loneliness is no longer there."

When God Speaks

Expanding their family has cost "Papa Elijah and Mama Ruth" both time and money. Though they consider it a blessing and not a sacrifice, time and again the Sebuchu's have used their personal savings to pay for a child to attend school. They've denied their own children in order to purchase a bicycle for a pastor with a lengthy commute. They have refused their children more than one pair of shoes because so many orphans had none. And at a time when they had barely enough for themselves, two homeless women benefited from their generosity . . .

"Hope" and "Peace"

Solomy[40] considers the comfort and significance of her life today in contrast to her days on the streets, when her daily goal was survival. She believes God used Pastor Elijah and his ministry to save her life.

Thrown to the streets after her parents died, Solomy sought escape at her brother's home, but was soon kicked out. She moved from one friend's apartment to another for a while, but before long, she was out of options. Homeless and desperate, she walked deep into the jungle and cried out to God during a three-day fast. It was her last resort.

At the end of three days, the phone she had borrowed rang. It was Pastor Elijah. News of Solomy had reached him. He sent a car to bring her back to the

---

[40] Solomy" comes from the Hebrew word "shalom" meaning *peace*.

church. Now, Solomy serves as sponsorship coordinator at Hands of Love, arguably the most important role of the ministry.

Allen Hope first met Elijah after she had been beaten and disowned by her father then cast out onto the streets of Kampala. Bruised and homeless, she attended Ruth and Elijah's church at a friend's invitation. There she found not just a place to worship, but also a safe place to sleep and, ultimately, a future.

Today, Hope serves with top-notch efficiency as part of the communication team. Elijah has witnessed a total transformation in Hope's life.

"Elijah and Ruth, they are not selfish," Hope says. "The little they get, they share with others. When I had nothing, they didn't have all that much to give. Yet they provided for me and shared what they had. They allowed me to sleep at the church. They denied their own children the best things in order to share with others. They inspire me every day."

But of all the Sebuchu's gave, she most appreciated finding a family with a "father" who recognized her true worth. Pastor Elijah saw potential in Allen Hope far beyond what she saw in herself. "There were times I wondered if I'd be able to meet his expectations. I thank God I have been able!"

When God Speaks

Solomy shares Hope's attitude of gratitude. Like Hope, Solomy has experienced the blessing of serving with purpose. In a single day, she wears hundreds of hats. From escorting a child to the airport where he'll meet his sponsor parents to comforting an HIV-infected child who has just arrived at the orphanage. With each interaction, Solomy transfers the joy and compassion of Jesus. She doesn't *talk* about Jesus that often. But when you're with her, you see the love of Christ in action. Fortunately for all who fall into the wake of her love, it's contagious.

Solomy (in the blue) with a Hands of Love student

But loving 2,600 children contagiously is still exhausting work. Solomy and many of the other "servants" put in six-day weeks, often finishing their work well past midnight. Some walk miles, spending two to three hours each day commuting by foot from their homes to the orphanage. (After all, a bicycle is a luxury.) To arrive at the orphanage in time to prepare their classrooms, most teachers start their days before the sun rises.

Still, Solomy rarely counts the cost. She thrives on the pace and demands of her job—correction—her *calling*.

"It has brought back the joy I once lost. When I serve these children, I feel happy. Before I met Pastor Elijah, I used to want to help people. I had suffered so much and saw others suffering in the same way. I felt pity for them but had no way to help them. This ministry has enabled me to do something more than just have pity."

Elijah and Ruth's generosity rippled the waters of Hope and Solomy's lives. The powerful waves they created are still being felt today.

"In 1998, we took Solomy in, even though we didn't have enough food for our family. She had been thrown out of her brother's home with nothing. I wish people would understand that when you reach out with hands of love and you touch a life, *just one life*, you sow a seed. That seed grows and will eventually touch the entire world. When I watch how Solomy serves—how many nights she goes without sleep for the sake of the children—I see how touching one life will touch millions."

The Unlikelies

Throughout history God has raised up the broken, poor, disheveled, and messiest lives to do His greatest work. It is no different at Hands of Love. God is still using the Allen Hope's and the Solomy's—those who've been cast out—to reach the outcast. He heals the broken and uses them, redeeming lives to reach those who also need healing.

When Allen Hope first came to Hands of Love, she was painfully shy and easy to overlook. There was nothing special or compelling about her outward appearance or behavior. Some doubted her leadership qualifications and were surprised when Elijah singled her out to fill an integral role in the ministry.

When God Speaks

"Elijah chooses his staff in an unconventional way," says Anna Latshaw, founder of Hands of Love USA. "Some might say it's contrary to good business sense."

But he is not concerned with what makes sense. He is concerned with whom God has called. Allen Hope and many other staff were chosen this way. God selected them and Elijah was obedient to whom He called.

Anna's story wasn't any different. "I'm a bit of an Allen Hope in a way," Anna says. When Elijah visited her Georgia home in 2007, he saw past her limited time as a stay-at-home mom with four small children and recognized Anna's passion and potential. At the time, there was no established presence for Hands of Love in America. But the vision-bearer sensed God stirring the young mother's heart. He boldly invited Anna to launch an initiative to support the network of orphanages by securing American sponsors.

"Even with four young kids, my limited availability, inexperience, and limited gifting, he didn't question any of that. Surely there was someone better, more qualified. But he never communicated any sense of that. I took it for granted at the time. But God led Elijah and Ruth in that decision."

Through tireless servanthood, working countless late nights, Anna's grass-roots efforts blossomed. Today Hands of Love USA is a national 501(c)(3) ministry with two full-time staff, an active board of directors and board of advisors. Hands of Love Foundation has dynamic partnerships throughout dozens of states. Through Anna's relational fund raising and partnerships, child sponsorships have grown from seventy-eight children in

2009 to over 1,000 as of this book's printing. The ambitious goal is to secure a sponsor for every child at the orphanages and to take in as many more thousands as resources will allow.

Some say their goal is too ambitious. But Elijah, Ruth, and their host of unlikely servants are not interested in going fast. They're interested in *going far*. One sponsor at a time, they do what they're called to do, and, eventually, the work will be done.

Carving Angels

Sometimes, when the day is long and the ocean of need is immense, the servant leaders at Hands of Love need to be reminded. Reminded of what they are doing.

Elijah's words and actions inspire his staff. Like an artist, he sculpts leaders who own the truth that they are causing transformation. From the cooks, to the house moms, to the principals, he compels each one to remember why they serve. He reminds them they are vision bearers.

"Many, many children in Uganda grow up as I did," Elijah says. "They have endured the poverty and many have been subject to the same violence of rebel and government soldiers. These children and many of our staff, have suffered in this way. Our staff have been handpicked by God to help many children get through what I went through. Some may not have been through all of it, but, to some extent, they have all suffered."

When God Speaks

Coaxing leaders out of broken vessels is one of Elijah's specialties. He looks at broken people and sees masterpieces-in-the-making. Michelangelo is quoted as saying, "I saw the angel in the marble and carved until I set him free." Elijah also sculpts "angels," but not with a hammer and chisel. Instead the mighty man of God fills his toolbox with prayer and fasting, biblical truth, and words of encouragement.

"When you are a vision bearer, you won't succeed until you cause the vision to be owned by the people who serve with you. You share the vision in such a way that those serving with you become owners of the same vision. My mom did this. She shared her vision of my life so that I would own it. It is mine now."

*****

The vision began with a seed of hope planted in a mother's heart as she held baby Elijah. The God of the impossible cast a vision of a boy who would change lives. The mother cast the vision to her son, who grew up believing it.

Fifty years later, the son looks on a boy eating from a trash heap and sees a future president of Uganda. He looks into the eyes of a child searching for his purpose. He sees the child through the God-of-the-Impossible lens. Because it just may be this child who saves Uganda from abject poverty or eradicates the HIV/AIDS problem.

It will not be Elijah, but it could be one of these children.

His methods mimic those of a God who specializes in finding life in dead zones. Hands of Love children are loved and educated. Seeds are planted and leaders grow.

> *"Blessed is the man who trusts in the Lord. And whose trust is the Lord. For he will be like a tree planted by the water, that extends its roots by a stream and will not fear when the heat comes; But its leaves will be green, and it will not be anxious in a year of drought, nor cease to yield fruit"*
>
> *(Jeremiah 17:8).*

When God Speaks

When God Speaks
The Beauty of a Servant

Solomy takes not one breath for granted. She views her life through the lens of grace. Gratitude overshadows her; it flows through each interaction with every child. I hear it in her laughter as she whispers translated Lugandan words to our sponsored son.

"Samuel, your mum wants to tell you something."

I watch him fight back tears. A golf-ball sized lump lodges itself in my throat. Inside the ministry van, sadness envelopes the back seat as we drive to the airport. I hate good-byes and, apparently, so does Samuel.

"Your mum says you are her very special boy and she is going to write to you." Solomy's voice is soft and sing-songy. "She is going to pray that God will bring them back to Uganda. Maybe God will let your whole family come next time. But, until then, you must promise her to work very hard in school and read your Bible every day. God loves you so much. That is why He sent your mum and dad to visit you."

Samuel nods and stares at his shoes. Solomy bought them from a local shoe peddler with the fifty-dollar monthly gift we send to Uganda. He fingers the watch that used to belong to his American brother, Owen. It has lived on his arm since he carefully removed it from the gift bag on day two of our trip.

An oncoming headlight beam moves across the van. In the dark, I glimpse his face. A tear slides down his cheek.

I squeeze his hand. Solomy smiles, radiates joy. Her smile ushers a flood of hope into the car and the sadness begins to drown. It's no wonder that the literal translation of her name is "peace."

I am buoyed by her presence and wonder if Samuel feels it too.

She whispers more Luganda. Though the words are foreign to me, I listen to the beauty of a servant speaking hope into a young child. Samuel nods his head. He wipes his tear and I see it: the corner of his mouth turning up. I'm comforted to know that this servant is going to love my son while I'm 7,500 miles away. This lovely servant of God will celebrate his birthday and another will bandage his knee when he scrapes it. Another will spoon posho into his bowl and another will teach him the truth of God's Word until we meet again.

I take comfort knowing he is in good hands. Servant hands.

Hands of love.

When God Speaks

Hands and Feet

You hear the phrase often in church, "we are the hands and feet of Jesus." I hear the words, imagine what that looks like, and let the idea sink in. But when I *do* the words, they sink in a lot deeper.

I remember a time I was served by the "hands of Christ." Twenty weeks into my third pregnancy, the ultrasound technician stared blankly at the screen. No heartbeat. The news crashed into me like a hurricane hits a beach front home. My plans for a third child—daughter number two—imploded in a matter of seconds.

The baby shower my girlfriends held the week before left behind a bounty of reminders. Reminders I didn't need. I closed the door to the room with the baby gifts, knowing at some point I'd have to open that door to yet another wave of grief.

But the hands and feet of Jesus tiptoed in the next day. They came quietly, removed the gifts, and returned them to *Babies 'R Us*, without pomp or circumstance.

Servant hands do difficult things. They do things that soften the blows of life. I want to do the hard things that make the days a bit less dreadful for the hurting. I want to serve in ways that matter most. I want to sacrifice like Elijah's family did for Hope and Solomy and return unused baby bottles for grieving mommas. I want to serve with the heart of a Savior who did the most difficult thing. He gave the most sacrificial gift so that we could carry His heart to "the least of these."

How might you walk in Jesus' shoes and *do* the things we talk about doing? The ripple effect just might surprise you. It could change more than the lives of others. It could change yours too.

> I slept and dreamt that life was joy.
> I awoke and saw that life was service.
> I acted and behold, service was joy.
> *[Rabindranath Tagore]*

8

Empowering the Next Generation

Cheers erupt as a black-and-white bull is escorted through the schoolyard and tied to a post behind the kitchen. He may be the least excited participant of Hands of Love's week-long celebration. The orphanage is buzzing with anticipation. Preparations are underway. Teachers print certificates of achievement for primary seven students.[41] Nimble hands pound large drums as Hands of Love dancers stomp to the rhythm. Students step to the beat rehearsing a traditional Ugandan dance for tomorrow morning's parade through the streets of Kampala.

The sound of tires on the gravel drive alerts Principal Sarah of the local news team's arrival. It's her second TV interview today. She straightens her white blouse, clears her throat, and mentally reviews her talking points one last time.

The children at Hands of Love are tomorrow's champions. Every one of these children has a purpose. Our sponsors and teachers make it possible for children—many of whom were formerly living on the streets—to obtain the best possible education. When we learned of our number five ranking out of 48,000

---

[41] Primary seven is equivalent to sixth grade in the US.

schools, we were very pleased. The hard work has paid off. Now it's time to celebrate!

Principal Sarah and the other staff and children are celebrating the school's second consecutive top-five national ranking. The rankings are a result of the Primary Seven students' performance on Uganda's Final Primary Living Examinations. Hands of Love children (in the US equivalent of sixth grade) sat with students from 48,000 other Ugandan schools for the exams, which are required for promotion into secondary school. Similar to US standardized tests, each child in Uganda, whether attending private or public school, is required to pass this exam. Not only did all Hands of Love students pass, they excelled. The school is currently the fifth highest ranked primary school in the entire nation of Uganda! And, it's no surprise that Hands of Love teachers have been recognized as the best in the nation.

Thomas

Outstanding schools produce outstanding students. Sixteen-year-old Thomas is a whiz. In fact, his exam scores earned him a top fifteen national ranking and number one among all primary seven students in his district. One of the original 188, Thomas came to Hands of Love as another of Uganda's countless AIDS orphans. He has been raised at the orphanage and doesn't remember his parents or know their names. What he does remember about his life before Hands of Love is the hunger that accompanied homelessness.

When God Speaks

"I would get so hungry when I lived in the bush. It was very difficult for me to find food. I survived on mangos, jackfruit, oranges, and other food. I would fetch water in the rivers but I got sick because the water was so contaminated. I didn't have shoes then, but now I do. If not for Pastor Elijah and Pastor Ruth, I never would have survived," Thomas says.

"Here I have a family and people who take care of me. We learn about God. That means I have a bright future." Thomas' sponsor family has generously invested in his future. In fact, they have committed to paying for Thomas' college education.

"I want to become a doctor because I want to treat my people who are suffering in this country. There is abject poverty in our country, high spread of diseases, and HIV/AIDS. Lots of suffering people are facing this. There are no doctors in these rural areas. People here are just living an unhappy life. They are poor. They are uneducated and work rural jobs. They have no money for doctors or medicine and they suffer. They use herbs from the bush. I want to become educated so I can come back and serve my people to give them a higher standard of living and a better future."

Two Heads are Better Than One

Whenever Berta smiles, you'd swear someone flipped on a light switch. Everything around her becomes brighter. And like those stars that shine brighter in dark skies, her smile is even more powerful amidst the backdrop of darkness she has overcome.

When God Speaks

Berta's father died when she was five, leaving her mother in a desperate situation. Her mother soon remarried in an attempt to improve her family's future. For a short time, Berta was able to attend school, but things took a drastic turn when Berta turned twelve.

"When I was twelve, my stepfather tried to rape me. I couldn't manage that situation, so I ran away from home. I went to live with my cousin." The young woman agreed to take Berta in as long as she served as her housemaid. "So I lived with her," Berta says. "But life was not simple."

Berta's complicated life included many "strings" attached to her job as housemaid. The twelve-year-old girl did every stitch of work required to run the household, including all cooking, cleaning, laundry, and childcare. In return, Berta was given only a place to sleep. Her cousin didn't feed or clothe her. To make matters worse, her cousin's husband made inappropriate sexual advances toward her.

"My cousin refused to give me food. I was doing all the chores while in pain from hunger. She would feed herself and her children but give me nothing." Berta survived by sneaking leftovers from the family's plates while washing dishes.

One day, Berta begged her cousin to allow her to attend school. She refused. "You are too old to go back to school," her cousin said. "You are just a refugee." Berta changed her tactics and, weeks later, asked if she could attend church. She was again denied. But Berta was persistent and her persistence eventually wore her cousin down. That first week of church, she attended

When God Speaks

Kampala International Christian Centre (KICC), where a tall, joyful pastor named Elijah greeted her.

"Pastor Elijah welcomed me so much. After I left that day, I knew there was someone who loved me. His welcome encouraged me to go back the next Sunday. When I returned home that day, my cousin threw me out. Pastor Elijah allowed me to come to Hands of Love, and I finally began learning."

Knowing that people in America might hear her story ignites a smile across Berta's face. Once again, she lights the room. And it is contagious.

"I send greetings to all the people in America! I love them because they have loved us. They help us to forget all our bad backgrounds. Please don't forget our stories."

Like Thomas and many others, Berta dreams of how her top-notch education will transform Uganda. "There are many children in Uganda on the streets. But, I have hope in my future. When I become rich, my first project will be to work together with Pastor Elijah, because he loves children. And together, we can help those street children. We will join our efforts because two heads are better than one. In addition to helping children, I want to become a doctor and I will treat the children in the community."

A Living Nightmare

Many of the children's stories begin the same: "I lost both my parents to AIDS."

Fifteen-year-old Gloria lost hers to the disease when she was a toddler. She went to live with her aunt at age four, but by the time Gloria turned nine, the woman couldn't afford to pay for school. Her aunt's solution was the next nightmare in a series of horrific experiences Gloria would endure as an orphan.

"My aunt arranged for a man to marry me," Gloria says, "but that man was thirty-eight years old. I was nine. I felt so bad, because it was wrong. So I decided to run away from home. I didn't have anywhere to go."

This all-too-common scene left the young girl homeless, searching for food and security. She made the decision to escape to the bush where she foraged for food and water. She would drink any she could find, whether clean or dirty.

"Sleeping in the bush was so scary. There were many wild animals. One day a lion came and tried to eat me. So, I climbed a tree and I hid."

Once, while "wandering from nowhere to nowhere" in the jungle, searching for something to eat, Gloria was greeted by an old woman who asked if she had food. Confessing that she hadn't eaten in days, Gloria followed the crooked-backed lady home. She stayed with her for two days.

One night, vivid images from her dreams harassed her. She tossed and turned. But in the middle of the night, she awoke into a living nightmare more gruesome than any bad dream her subconscious fears could conjure.

*****

When God Speaks

Gloria thrashed about on the thin mattress where she slept. Sweat beaded her forehead. A man with a large machete was chasing her. "I will get you!" he screamed. She tried to run but her cement legs were useless. He closed in on her, reaching for her dress. Just as his fingers slipped through the fabric, she screamed. She opened her eyes. Her breath was stuck in her lungs. She reached for her throat and gasped for air. Her damp dress clung to her fear-frozen body.

She forced a steady stream of air through her lips and her pulse slowed a bit. After several minutes, the sleepy haze began to lift. She surveyed the dark room. She could barely make out its contents except for one simple chair in the corner and a small crate beside the bed. Memories of the day before slowly calmed the wake of her nightmare. A hunched old woman had given her *matooke*—her first food in two days—and brought her back here to rest.

The faster she calmed down and went back to sleep, the faster morning would come. But with sleep came the potential for more bad dreams. Maybe the old lady would let her sleep in her room. She arose, tiptoed out of her room, and searched the small house. No sign of her inside. Though she suspected the woman might be using the pit latrine, Gloria was still too scared to venture outside. Returning to bed, she sat upright, her legs trembling under her ragged skirt.

Suddenly a strange noise—a loud, whirring—sounded in the next room. Her pulse quickened. She imagined some otherworldly kind of gigantic insect hovering just a few yards away. Gloria listened for the old woman's steps but heard only the bizarre whir and the blood pounding in her ears.

When God Speaks

With every passing minute, Gloria's fear mounted. She focused hard, willing the woman to come back from the pit latrine and save her from whatever was looming outside her room. But she didn't come. Quietly, carefully, Gloria snaked under the bed, desperate to find some protection from the wild beast that might be prowling in the next room.

The front door creaked, then quick footsteps thumped by her door, much quicker than the old lady moved. Panic set in as Gloria recalled horrific stories she'd heard from other street orphans. Stories of demon possessions and witchcraft that she had always hoped were just made up. Right now she believed every word.

Sensing the need to rescue herself rather than depend on the old lady, Gloria inched her body out from under the bed, taking care not to make noise. Her sweaty palms slipped on the floor as she scooted closer to the door of the room where she hid. She peered through the door crack. At first, she struggled to see much of anything. She shifted her body slightly to the left and adjusted her gaze toward the right side of the room.

She gasped.

The old woman was no longer stooped over. She stood upright and moved swiftly up and down the hall. Gloria had heard witchcraft stories about evil spirits transforming old people and taking over their bodies to perform unthinkable acts. Cold fear enveloped the girl, sending shivers down her spine. Like blades of grass paralyzed by February's frost, every hair on her body stood erect.

When God Speaks

More footsteps came and then a door latched.

It was time to make her move. She crept into the next room and sunk down behind a wooden crate. She was one room closer to the front door. Peering out from behind the crate, Gloria scanned the hall that led to her freedom. As her eyes adjusted to the change in light, what she saw in the hall stopped her breathing.

Skeletons and dead bodies—mostly those of children—were piled haphazardly in a wooden box. Shock and terror sucked her breath away. She began to choke, but fear of being discovered quickly silenced her. A grotesque smell assaulted her nose. She gagged. A heap of torn, blood-stained children's clothing lay beside a pile of skulls.

She wanted to scream, but her vocal chords seized. Shaking uncontrollably, she tiptoed out of the room and hid behind a door. Something wet brushed the side of her neck. She realized she had been crying so hard, the collar of her blouse was damp.

Gloria stood watching from behind the door jamb. Her lower lip trembled violently. The lady buzzed about, moving as if she were twenty-four instead of eighty-four. She was carrying something on her shoulder but Gloria couldn't make it out.

Time seemed to slow as Gloria waited for the lady to leave the room again. As she mentally rehearsed the path to the door, she prepared for the run of her life.

When God Speaks

Again the door clicked shut. Gloria drew up her courage, shielded her eyes from the macabre hallway, and dashed out the front door. The lady turned in the girl's direction, but before she saw her, Gloria flew behind a large palm tree. She stood stone still for what seemed like hours. The lady studied the palm and even began walking toward Gloria. But something made her return to the house.

It was go time. Gloria raced from the palm tree. Her adrenaline-charged legs carried her in a hard sprint, away from the house, until she had no more breath to run. When she reached a small clearing in the bush, she slowed. All at once, her legs gave out. She dissolved onto the jungle floor, curling into the fetal position.

Tears came so hard she could barely catch air in between sobs. She cried from relief and for what she had seen. She cried for herself and for those dead children. She could have cried until the sun rose, but the bizarre bush noises sobered her long enough to rethink her sleeping arrangement.

She wiped her face with her blouse, straightened, and walked toward a massive banyan tree with low limbs. She began to climb. Climbing trees was something she could normally do in her sleep, but, tonight, reaching the next limb seemed a hundred times harder than ever before. Exhausted and still shaking, she willed herself higher and higher. She wanted to climb to the stars to escape this living nightmare, but the tree wasn't that tall.

When God Speaks

Gloria found the widest, highest branch and laid down, carefully balancing her long legs. For a while, fear held her eyes wide open, but, eventually, exhaustion won the battle. Her eyelids gave way and she slept.

Deliverance

Deliverance came later the next morning. After wandering the bush, Gloria reached a group of women and children who were farming. One of the women asked where she was coming from. Still shaken from her last encounter with a stranger, she began to walk away. The woman called after her and told her not to fear. Something about her voice seemed trustworthy. The lady began asking her about her background and, bit by bit, Gloria opened up. The woman's children assured Gloria that things would get better. For some reason, Gloria believed them.

Little did Gloria know, the stranger was a Hands of Love foster mom. The children she fostered attended school at Hands of Love and lived with her in the evenings. Eventually she took Gloria to Pastor Elijah, who reviewed her background and admitted her to the orphanage.

"When I came here six years ago, I no longer felt I was an orphan," Gloria says. "The love shown to me was the most important thing. And having a sponsor."

A few years after Gloria came to Hands of Love, an American couple from Atlanta Georgia visited the orphanage. During their stay, they watched Gloria and the other children perform with the Hands of Love choir.

"When they saw me sing and dance, they chose me to be their daughter. They became my parents that day. I thank them so much for having chosen me from among all the other children. May God bless them so much.

"I want others to know that sponsoring children is so important. If you choose to sponsor a child, God will bless you. The decision to sponsor lets that child know that there is someone else who loves them. It helps children believe that they can live in good conditions rather than be orphans."

Staff members encourage Gloria and all the children at Hands of Love to set and reach specific goals. "When I finish up my studies, I want to be an international journalist and a musician. Journalists discover many things. I want to discover so much in my life, so I've decided to pursue journalism. I also think I'm talented in singing."

Thanks to Hands of Love, Thomas, Berta, Gloria, and hundreds of other vulnerable children have experienced the healing of being chosen. Though many of them have been through horrific experiences—starvation, abuse, eating trash, being chased by sacrificers, witnessing cannibalism, even being kidnapped—love's transforming effect is undeniable. In fact, it's downright miraculous.

"The world has millions of people who are love-starved. Nothing kills people quicker than a person being love-starved. When you love your children," Elijah reminds, "you will have prepared them to be lovers of people and established a fertile ground in their lives to be loved."

When God Speaks

Unfortunately, due to lack of resources, the orphanage is unable to provide an abundance of food for all the children. Many children remain without sponsors, which means they lack the complete nutrition sponsored kids receive. To feed the unsponsored kids, European and American missionaries donate meals, and generous partners like Convoy of Hope provide nutritious manna packs[42]. But what's lacking in food is made up for in heaping servings of love.

Being love-starved is far worse than being food-starved and there is no shortage of love at this oasis of joy.

I Like to Build Things

A child raised in a poverty-ridden, polygamous culture faces a multitude of challenges. Nineteen-year-old Joseph endured a childhood plagued with frequent disputes between his father's three wives. After contracting HIV/AIDS, his parents became a statistic like many others in polygamous families. His mom, dad, and one stepmother died, leaving only the third wife. Joseph had no choice but to live with the angry, desperate woman. She started beating him, demanding harsh labor without offering food.

---

[42] Convoy of Hope is a faith-based organization that feeds millions of hungry people across the world. In 2019 the organization donated 40 tons of super-food, worth hundreds of thousands of dollars, to the Namadhi and Kabaga-Kampala orphanages.

When God Speaks

"I would dig for my stepmom from the time I woke until 2 p.m. When I finished, she would not give me food, only her own children. She told me that if I wanted to eat, I must fetch five *jerricans* of water. So, I would do it. When she gave me food it was so little it wasn't enough to sustain me," he says.

One day Joseph's stepmom called him to go work in the fields. He was ill and could barely stand, but still she forced him to go. At some point during the day, Joseph passed out from fatigue. The woman saw him "being lazy" and beat him until he again passed out.

"She beat me so hard that she almost killed me. She left me to die in the garden. Many people were trying to stop her from mistreating me, but she would tell them 'You cannot force me. He is my child. Don't tell me what to do.'"

Mary, a woman from Joseph's village, witnessed the scene and carried him to her home. Later, his wicked stepmother lied to Mary. "Joseph is just a lazy boy. He was laying down on the job." Mary believed her, promptly gave Joseph another beating, and told him to get to work in her home. The abuse continued until he ran away to a friend's home.

Eventually, Joseph became a nomad. He landed in the bush where he foraged for fruit. He stole cassava (similar to potatoes) and ate them raw because he had no way to cook. "I was so hungry. I was very lonely and very afraid. There wasn't anywhere to get water," says Joseph.

During his stay in the jungle, Joseph met an unwelcomed guest. "As I was sleeping, a huge snake—a python—surrounded me. He wrapped himself around me. I awoke, grabbed a huge stick and beat it until it let go of me. I was in terrible condition."

While running from the reptile, Joseph impaled his foot on a sharp stick. The nasty wound grounded him for three days. Hurt, hungry, and alone, Joseph was in desperate need of a miracle.

After three days of being stranded in the bush, a herdsman grazing his animals found Joseph asleep. He was a kind man, and he carried Joseph back to his home, nursed his wound, and shared the household food. But after two weeks, the herdsman's mother accused the boy of stealing clothes and demanded he leave.

Joseph hadn't taken a thing.

His situation remained grim until, one day, Joseph's path was divinely crossed with a stranger's at the village trading center. The man was a friend of the Hands of Love's headmaster. Later that day, the two visited headmaster Joseph. After hearing the boy's story, he was admitted to the orphanage.

That was five years ago, "the first time since my parents died that I received an education. I am now safe. People here are very kind. I don't have a sponsor, but I have food. Life is better now compared to where I came from."

Joseph's new life has motivated him to set goals. "I want to become an engineer. I like to put things together. I want to build things," he says.

When God Speaks

The Most Important People in Uganda

When these champions speak of building, advocating, and transforming Uganda, I see the spark that has been ignited by their Hands of Love "family." As they share their dreams and goals, I read between the lines and hear hope's whisper: *I am worth something. Someone out there loves me. I know, because they chose me.*

Even the unsponsored ones believe they are chosen . . . by God. They have worth whether or not they have a sponsored mom or dad, because they have a Heavenly Dad whose provision blows away any on earth. No investment portfolio can compare to the storehouses of heaven. But because of their horrific backgrounds, some have a harder time grasping this truth. Elijah and his team of servant leaders must work and pray extra hard to remind them.

*****

Elijah stands before hundreds of sponsored and unsponsored kids at the Namadhi orphanage. He introduces my husband and me, then gives an important reminder. "My big friends from South Carolina came a very long way to meet you, because you are the most important people in Uganda."

He then equips them with future-building truth. "You are not ordinary children. Every one of you are going to grow up and you are going to become big people. Important people. You are going to become powerful! You will not be poor! You will not die of AIDS! You are going to change everything! Change everything!"

When God Speaks

Up front, a tiny boy sits on his knees and fiddles with dusty toes. A word catches his attention. He stops, looks up at Elijah, and tunes in. "In Uganda, we have only 8 doctors per 100,000 people serving a country of over 45 million. Seated here before me today, there are future doctors. There are many corrupt lawyers in Uganda, but seated here," he says, pointing to the champions, "there are lawyers who will *not* be corrupt. Many pastors in Uganda cannot even read English. They are not educated. But some of you educated children will become pastors. Many of our mothers in villages here cannot even write their name. You are going to be mothers . . . and fathers . . . and pilots and teachers. And some of you will grow up and help the millions of children outside our gates who have no education." As Elijah speaks, I watch their faces.

And I see sparks igniting.

Together

As an evangelist, church planter, and director of an international foundation, Elijah signs thousands of letters a month. I love how he signs them. Instead of ending with "Sincerely Yours" or "God bless you," his recipients receive a promise:

"Together we can make all the difference."

This ingenious slogan is both a promise and a challenge. One that isn't simply words above his name or a flippant phrase on his tongue. It's what Elijah lives. The relationship-is-better-than-meat man has always believed two heads are better than one and a strand of three cords is not easily broken. He believes that one child at a time, an entire nation can be changed. To him, each child is precious and has purpose. The gift of just one sponsor can breathe life into a child and the ripple effects of that one resulting champion are astounding. He believes it all adds up to transformation in Uganda.

But "together" is the key word.

Together we can ignite sparks. Together we can share the message of empowered children who top Uganda's educational charts. Together we can challenge others to get their heads in the game.

Together.

When God Speaks

Tomorrow's Champions

I'm scrolling through Facebook one Saturday afternoon, chuckling as I watch two teenage kids dump buckets of ice cold water on their father's head. It's clear who put him up to the "ice bucket challenge" that promises to be one of the most astonishingly successful fundraising campaigns to date. Social media is a powerful tool in the hands of a purposeful person.

Take Will Hankins, for example. Fifteen-year-old Will traveled to both Hands of Love orphanages a few years ago with a team from Atlanta, Georgia. Will and his team hosted a Bible school camp which involved the children in crafts, games, songs, skits, and lessons. He played his ukulele and taught the kids how to play kickball. "But that turned into a game of soccer pretty quickly," Will says with a laugh. "They are *all* about soccer there."

But connecting with the kids and hearing their stories gave Will his biggest take-away. "Before Hands of Love, those kids were living out of trash cans. I think there is a certain joy that they have living there because of where they came from. I think the joy comes from knowing that there are people out there for *them*, that love them."

Looking into the children's eyes and hearing this first hand gave Will a strong sense of purpose. "I feel a responsibility and a duty to serve Hands of Love because I saw these people with my own eyes. I can't just say 'they are

8,000 miles away.' I feel obligated and I want to provide for them in any way I can."

"My trip to Uganda gave me a sense of purpose for better and for worse," he says. "When I got back, I viewed everything differently. A few days after he came home from Africa, he found his younger brother laying on the living room floor.

"Come on, mom!" Jackson whined. "What's the big deal if I bring one more friend to the water park? I don't want to leave anyone out."

Will's mind jogged back to the side of a road he had traveled in Uganda. Two small girls—maybe six or seven years old—squatted next to a muddy puddle. They took turns dipping their hands into the murky, brown water and taking sips.

"Give me a break, Jackson! There are tons of kids in Uganda who don't even have clean water to *drink*, let alone a thousand gallons to *waste* riding down a stinking water park slide. Give it a rest, dude!" Will stormed out the front door to find some fresh air.

I get Will's knee-jerk reaction to the incredible contrast in lifestyles between Uganda and the U.S. I've been there myself (and I'm sure many reading this have too.) I'm still tempted to lash out at my children when they complain that their quarter-pound hamburger is cooked medium, rather than medium-rare. Instead, I take a deep breath. "First-world problem," I tell them. And I silently thank God for the abundance of meat, fresh fruit and vegetables, and any other type of food we care to buy at the two-acre grocery store just outside my subdivision.

Will and I share these frustrations, but we also share a sense of purpose. Like those in the ice bucket challenge who reached out on social media, Will used Facebook, e-mail, and text messaging to extend a hand into Uganda's ocean of poverty. Soon after he came home, he launched an ambitious fundraising campaign on GoFundMe.com, challenging friends, family, and acquaintances to give to Hands of Love. He surpassed his $10,000 dollar goal by making personal contact. Because of Will's ripple effect, unsponsored children will receive much needed meals. The whopping $13,000 dollars he generated will greatly offset costly overseas shipping for manna packs[43] donated by Convoy of Hope.

Though Uganda's AIDS orphan epidemic is too immense for one person to tackle alone, "using that as a reason to do nothing is ridiculous logic," says Will. "And it's no way to get anything done. If everyone has that mindset the problems are going to get bigger. One person or 100,000 people can't solve all the problems overnight. But with fifty dollars a month, you can completely change *one* person's life." As Pastor Elijah says, "We can't do everything but we can all do something."

---

[43] Manna packs are enriched bundles of rice that are used to provide valuable nutrients to those who are malnourished.

"Queen" of the Girl Scouts

Girl Scout leader Michelle Augusta, is challenging her middle school scouts to make a difference in one very important life. The troop has agreed to partner with Hands of Love to cover education fees for fourteen-year-old, Queen, another child of Hands of Love. The troop will fundraise and do service projects to cover the monthly fee.

Queen's father took off and her mother fell sick, leaving her and her siblings without any food. Eventually a family member removed their mother from the home and the landlord discovered the abandoned children. He brought them to Hands of Love where they all live today.

Michelle believes her hand-extending girls can make a difference in Queen's life. In addition to financial support, the girl scouts will correspond with Queen. In return, Michelle hopes the first-world girls will gain much needed perspective from their third-world friend. "Just yesterday, my daughter's good friend and fellow Girl Scout informed me, 'your daughter's phone is embarrassing, and you need to get her an iPhone.' Michelle's daughter was being teased at school because of her outdated phone.

Michelle encourages the girls to think twice before indulging in luxuries such as designer purses, shoes, and the latest, greatest smart phone. "The newest iPhone, which retails for $900 dollars (not including the forty plus dollars per month for cell service) would buy fifteen-plus months of valuable education, food, and clothing in Uganda."

When God Speaks

When I think of Queen and her siblings, Gloria and the living nightmare, and Berta living off the kind of scraps I often feed my dog, I'm floored by the difference fifty dollars a month has made. And the impact of one teenage boy and one Girl Scout troop.

Will's trip to Uganda changed him. It gave him a get-off-the-couch sense of purpose. We'd do well to follow his lead. "There's always someone you can help no matter what. Put your mind to it. Get off the couch and you can pretty much do anything you set your mind to."

The ripple effects from hand extenders like Will are staggering. So staggering, they just might wake up the couch-sleepers. They just might wake up and decide not to change the channel, but to change the world.

9

Got Faith?

G igantic faith doesn't just happen. Throughout fifty-plus years of trusting and believing God, Elijah's faith has grown day by day and trial by trial. Rooted in his mother's prayers, his faith matured as God responded to his cries again and again, in the most desperate situations.

Gigantic faith "proves to the mind the reality of things that cannot be seen by the bodily eye[44]." When God tells Elijah to feed, educate, and empower *30,000* orphaned and abandoned children, he considers it as good as done. When God tells Elijah, "Move!" he does. His faith propels him to go, even when there is no logical, practical way to reach the destination.

Entertaining Angels

During the late 1990's, Elijah and Ruth were busy planting churches. One day, Elijah received an invitation to a large conference in Kenya. After seeking God's approval, Elijah told his friend, Pastor Robert Khawa[45], "I will go to Kenya. God is calling me to go there."

---

[44] Matthew Henry's Concise Commentary

[45] Khawa is Senior Pastor at Miracle Center Church in Jinja, Uganda.

When God Speaks

Though he had no money for the hefty bus fare and other transportation costs, he was determined to go. Time and again, God had proven himself faithful to Elijah. He knew this time would be no different. Pastor Robert specified that Elijah was responsible for raising the money for his own transport. And so, as the trip quickly approached, one question weighed heavy on the young pastor. *I know You will provide the money to get to Kenya. But how, God?*

The departure day came, and the two pastors arrived at the bustling Customs and Immigration Department Station on the border of Uganda and Kenya. Elijah's wallet was empty but his conviction to go to Kenya was abundant. As they stood in line to complete the immigration process, Pastor Robert turned to him.

"Are you sure you have money for the bus?"

"Yes I have it." Elijah answered as if God had already delivered on His promise. Because gigantic faith *acts* on God's promises, even *before* the promise is delivered.

There was a long line to process the Kenyan VISA required for his trip. With less than five dollars in his pocket, Elijah stood third in line to pay the five dollar fee. On his left, a mysterious woman approached him. She scrutinized Elijah like an art student examining a Boticelli fresco. Her eyes flashed a puzzled, wild look. As the next person moved up to the attendant, steadfast Elijah got out of line and reclaimed his position behind twenty others.

The odd woman vanished.

Pastor Robert shook his head. "Elijah! What is wrong with you?"

Elijah silently dropped his head and shoved his hands in his empty pockets. He continued his wait, until he was next. Again, he returned to the back of the line. *Pastor Robert must think I am insane. But I must wait on God.* A third time, Elijah repeated the insanity and resumed the last place in line.

Pastor Robert threw his head back. He closed his eyes in disbelief. "No! Are you out of your mind?"

For the fourth time Elijah waited in the long line behind the other travelers. Out of the corner of his eye, he recognized the same strange women who approached him before. This time, she was holding a small object—a paper bag. She walked directly to Elijah, shoved the bag into his hands, then dashed away as if being chased. As quickly as she came, she disappeared. Again.

A bit alarmed by taking possession of an odd bag with unidentified contents in a bus station at the border, Elijah scanned the area. His better judgment and experience with thieves urged him to find a private place before examining the contents. He spied a rest room and entered an open stall, closing the door in front of him.

Elijah felt adrenaline surging through his body like the flash floods that ravage Uganda's rainy-season roads. Exhaling deeply, his jittery hands slowly opened the bag. He peeked in. What he saw took his breath away.

When God Speaks

The bag was full of cash—bundles of cash[46]. Unable to contain himself, the formerly poor pastor fell to his knees and wept with joy. The God of the Impossible had paid his way to Kenya, with plenty left over.

An $85,000 Dollar Elephant

It's been fifteen years since the paper bag incident. I look at my watch for the seventeenth time. Pastor Elijah is running late today. My husband and I have grown accustomed to Uganda time. Here in Kampala, poor roads, horrible traffic, and a more relaxed approach to schedules often delay our meeting times by thirty minutes to an hour. But today, we have waited so long that our minds jump to various conclusions. We people watch, check e-mail and Facebook, update our travel blog, and watch the news report blaring in the hotel lobby.

Still no Elijah.

As the third hour of our wait begins, we hear a vehicle approaching. I crane my neck, peering out the glass doors to see if it's him. Elijah walks into the hotel lobby with arms wide open. We stand to receive his warm embrace and sincere apology.

"Oh my friends! Oh my friends, my apologies for your wait. Please. Let us sit down for a moment." Elijah gestures toward a pair of couches; uneasiness

---

[46] Elijah was so overcome with shock that he failed to count the money for an exact sum. He estimates the bag contained approximately $8,000 US dollars.

creases his dark eyes. He seems a bit off today. We listen as he explains his delay.

"I am very sorry to have to share this news with you. A child from the Kabaga-Kampala Hands of Love school was abducted this morning.

Elijah's words careen into our quiet morning like a wrecking ball. Was it her tiny hand that I high-fived during yesterday's welcome celebration?

"Some people snuck past our security guards," Elijah explains, "and they grabbed her." The police were notified and, praise God, the girl was later found and hospitalized. She was deeply traumatized and received treatment for shock and drug injections.

Pain etches each word. We are accustomed to being fed life-giving words from this pastor's mouth. But these words gag. We choke on the bitter reality of the despair that surrounds Hands of Love, just outside its walls. A desert filled with desperate people, so desperate that stealing and sacrificing children is a common source of income.

As shepherd and overseer of their flock of children, Elijah and Ruth have made hard choices. They've chosen not to sleep in a hut when 188 children came and there wasn't room for all to have shelter. Instead, they chose to sleep in the open, subjecting themselves to wild animals, insects, and the elements. They chose to educate rather than clothe. They chose to stop accepting more orphans to focus on finding sponsors for those without. Every day, limited resources dictate hundreds of painful choices.

When God Speaks

But of all these choices, the most difficult involve the children's security.

"Insecurity is a very big issue here," Elijah says. "The children at Hands of Love know that once a kidnapper gets a child, they either sacrifice him or ask for ransom. Can you imagine the pain? This is a child rescued from the streets, you have been with that child for many years. He is now healthy and looking good. He has big dreams, to be a lawyer who advocates for the helpless. Then, one day, he gets kidnapped. That brings a lot of pain!"

But tight security has a high price tag in Uganda. To construct a proper security wall around one orphanage costs more than $85,000 US dollars. Elijah can feed, clothe, and educate a lot of children for that kind of money. Despite the morning's tragic events, he and the other leadership make the difficult choice to use their resources on other essentials. Then, they pray without ceasing for God's protection, encourage staff to be extra vigilant, and share the need with people like us.

Elijah doesn't have $85,000 dollars of disposable income. But what he does have is gigantic faith in the God of the Impossible. So he leaves the request for a security wall in the hands of his all-powerful God. The very same God who delivered him from the mouth of a lion.

And his daughter from the hands of kidnappers . . .

Kidnapped

It was Christmas time, and Elijah and his family were busy with holiday rehearsals and other preparations. Esther, Elijah's daughter, was scheduled to leave home at 1 p.m. for choir practice. Typically, Ruth was her daughter's designated driver, but she was occupied elsewhere. So Esther hired a motorcycle driver to take her to Kiteezi where she would hail a taxi to reach their church.

*****

Esther glanced at her watch and scanned the busy Kiteezi street located a few miles from Kampala. She hated to be late to choir practice. Suddenly a car appeared. "Just in time," she said under her breath. As she approached the taxi, she noticed three men in front: a driver, a young man on the passenger side, and a smaller man sandwiched in between.

She opened the door just as another woman holding a small baby approached the car from the other side. The three new passengers climbed into the back seat, shut the doors, and off they went.

"Where to?" The gruff driver shot a questioning look at Esther via the rearview mirror.

"Kampala International Christian Centre." She gave him the address.

He nodded and asked for the other passenger's destination. It was a fairly quiet ride. There was an occasional honk of the horn when streams of pedestrians blocked the driver's way, but Esther hardly noticed. She hummed the Christmas worship set in her head, tapping her fingers to the beat.

The car slowed as they approached the corner of the drive that led to KICC, the Sebuchu's home church and Esther's stop.

Esther checked her watch again. She had one minute to make it down the drive to the church.

"I will get off here, sir!" She began gathering her belongings and reached for the door handle.

The automatic locks clicked.

Esther tried the handle. It wouldn't budge. "Please, sir! Unlock the door? This is my stop." She jiggled the handle again, applying more force. It was locked tight. The car sped up. She shot a glance at the mother, who clutched her baby to her bosom, looking as anxious as Esther felt.

"Hey! You must stop! I am going to scream louder if you do not stop. Stop!" Esther's heart raced faster than the speeding car. "Stop!!" she screamed as loudly as she could.

The man in the passenger seat jerked around. His cold, dark eyes bore into hers, and he spat as he yelled. "Shut up, stupid girl! We are going to kill you if you keep shouting!"

The man in the middle laughed and muttered something to the driver, then cursed and laughed some more.

Esther reached for the woman's hand. She shook with fear. The woman pulled her hand away and clung to the door handle. Esther wondered if she too was considering jumping out the window. But fear won out and no one moved.

At top speed, the taxi was hurling down a street that led out of town into the bush. The back-seat captives sped away from the places and people Esther knew best. Away from her home, her neighbors, and her church. And far, far away from the police.

The afternoon light faded and the surrounding vegetation grew more and more dense. Esther's mind jumped to frightful conclusions of how the crazy men would get rid of her. She felt her pulse rate increase as the worry grew into panic. Out of nowhere she heard a whisper.

"Pray," a voice said.

She looked at the woman. "Excuse me?" But the woman was zoned out, staring silently into the night with tears running down her face.

"Pray." The "voice" was like a thought but it wasn't hers.

She began to pray silently. *Help me Jesus. Help me Jesus. Father, You are in charge of the Universe and You are able to save me. Save me from these wicked men. Save me, Jesus. Please save me."* Esther's silent prayer rose to heaven. The three-word response that came next was her ticket out of this living hell.

"Scream my name," the familiar voice said.

When God Speaks

Esther began screaming. "Jesus! Jesus! Save me, Jesus!" The startled baby began to wail.

"Shut up!" the men grew more and more agitated. They cursed and shouted, ordering her to stop. But Esther continued imploring Jesus to save her.

The car screeched to a halt. The woman lurched forward so hard Esther thought the baby was going to fall on the floor, but she grabbed the howling infant in time. The "taxi driver" opened the front door, jumped out from behind the wheel, and yanked open Esther's door. She was face to face with her captor. There was only one thing to do.

With her last shred of courage, Esther looked her kidnapper square on, took a deep breath, and let out her loudest cry yet. JESUS...... "Jeeeeeeeeeeessssssssuuuuuuus!"

The man reached into the car. Grabbed her left arm and jerked her out onto the ground. Esther lay face down in shock, repeating her Savior's name under her breath. "Jesus . . . Jesus . . ."

She didn't dare look up. She braced herself for the worst and kept murmuring "Jesus." But no beating came. Instead, she heard a car door slam. She slowly lifted her head and watched as the car sped away. As quickly as they had appeared, her kidnappers had vanished.

When God Speaks

Waging War

Back at Elijah's house, the family reassembled. Ruth supposed choir rehearsal had run long, but with every passing minute, her worry grew. She questioned Elijah but he had been working in his KICC office and hadn't seen his daughter at church (which was not unusual for the busy pastor).

Finally, Esther's brother, Meshach, returned from his activities. "No, Daddy. I never saw my sister at church today," Meshach said.

Elijah phoned Solomy still hoping there had been a mix-up. Solomy's response came like a kick in his gut. "No, Pastor. I've not seen Esther all day." Elijah embraced his wife and they dropped to the floor. The couple cried out to God to save Esther. They waged war on their knees, declaring life over their daughter and dismantling the schemes of the evil one in the mighty name of Jesus Christ. The two parents prayed for what seemed like an hour. Then Ruth's phone began to ring.

The calls kept getting disconnected, but eventually Elijah was able to answer. A woman's voice blared through the line. "Hello? Is this Pastor Elijah Sebuchu?"

"Yes, I am Pastor Elijah."

"There is a young woman here lying on the ground. She collapsed after trying to call you many times."

Elijah nearly dropped the phone but recovered his fumble and confirmed the woman's exact location: Kampala City Center. Next, he and Ruth notified their security guard who rushed the couple to City Center. Never before had they been more desperate to get across town. The fifteen-minute car ride seemed endless, but they finally pulled up to a large crowd. The pastors rushed out and pushed through the horde. Reaching the center, they looked down. Lying on her back, with closed eyes, was their teenage daughter. She was alive and appeared unharmed.

Though she was unconscious and in shock, after several hours, Esther came back to consciousness. She remembered the entire kidnapping and even shared details with her daddy later that morning. Her most vivid memory was how the name of Jesus saved her.

"If only people would understand," Elijah says, "the power that is in the name of Jesus, this world would be a much better place. The name of Jesus has power to make a barren womb fertile and to break down an orphan spirit. I always encourage people to call upon the name of Jesus. If people could grasp the power in this name, this world will be much better!"

Elijah and Ruth's response to Esther's kidnapping was faith in action. When they learned their daughter was missing, they prayed *first*. People with gigantic faith scream the name of Jesus in the face of evil men. They drop to their knees and call on God instead of calling 9-1-1.

But what kind of faith does it take to confront a different kind of enemy?

On his life's journey, Elijah faced physical threats, encountered witchcraft, and was chased by killers. But on his first trip to America, Elijah encountered a testing of faith like never before.

When God Speaks

The God of Uganda and the God of America

Just a few years after building the Hands of Love huts, Elijah received an exciting invitation. Saddleback Church's Senior Pastor, Dr. Rick Warren, invited the Ugandan Pastor to speak at the Global Summit on AIDS and The Church. Though friends had warned Elijah of America's corruption, he and Ruth prayerfully considered the request and felt God calling them to go.

Despite the fact that Elijah lacked money for airfare to America, their UK friends, John and Linda Gray, strongly urged him to go. On one of his subsequent UK visits, the Gray's extended a hand and introduced their Ugandan friend to Barrie and Eileen Jones[47]. The Jones offered to pay Elijah's round trip fare to Los Angeles and a lifelong friendship followed.

Elijah will never forget the day his plane landed in Los Angeles International Airport. As he disembarked, a mixture of shock and fear engulfed him. Sobbing, he dropped to his knees inside the airport gate. People stared at the skinny, black pastor kneeling face down in the waiting area. Couples whispered and pointed as Elijah continued to cry. He ignored the bystanders and gathered himself for an impromptu prayer session.

First, he asked God to protect him from the corruption of the West. He remembered his friends' words: "When someone strong in the Lord goes to

---

[47] In 2007, the Joneses introduced Elijah to their daughter, Anna Latshaw, who became the founder of Hands of Love USA six months later.

When God Speaks

America, they will become corrupt." But he also remembered what God told him: "You must go find American friends to serve the children."

"God," he prayed. "You created me, You saved me, and You own me. You have redeemed me though many, many things. Each incident was enough to kill me. The jiggers were enough to kill me. The hunger. The thirst. Measles. Diarrhea. Snakes. The lion. The bullets. The rebels. The walking for eighty miles. Sleeping in the jungles and the bush . . . Every one of these things could have taken my life. But Lord, you kept me for a purpose. Now Lord, I have arrived in America. Help me to never—at any time in my life—be corrupted by America. Some people may bribe me, tempting me to sell my ministry. But God, I want to build friendships here. Protect me from corruption, Lord."

Elijah's prayer continued for twenty minutes. He asked God for genuine relationships with honest people. He prayed for Americans to understand his number-one purpose: to build relationships, not to raise money. Eventually, the police approached and urged him to continue on his way.

As Elijah strolled through the airport, stood on the people mover, then boarded the bus, he observed the land of plenty. People driving shiny cars. Beautiful homes with green lawns. Paved roads with streetlights. Where were the crowds of barefooted pedestrians? The ramshackle storefronts? Where were the abandoned and starving children?

Remembering where he was just the day before, when he passed hungry children begging for food on his way to Kampala's Entebbe airport, Elijah wept. "God. I've served you for many, many years. But You can't be the God of

America—where even the beggars can become donors—and also the God of Uganda, where people are dying without food. No. You cannot be the same God."

The debate continued once he reached his hotel room where Elijah found not one, but two huge beds, wall-to-wall carpet, a kitchen with clean running water, and a coffeemaker. He couldn't believe his eyes, and he continued wrestling with the God of Uganda throughout the night. He refrained from eating and begged for an answer. "How can You let Uganda suffer while the people of America enjoy such excess?"

The bewildered pastor spent the next three days and nights in prayer and fasting. Surrounded by luxury, plenty of clean water, and abundant food, his hunger for God's answer once again took priority over his physical hunger.

On the third day, God spoke.

"Elijah, I am the God you have served for all these years. I am the same God of Uganda. And the same God of America. I am the God who has blessed this nation of America with more than enough, more than what they need, that they might be a blessing to the rest of the world."

That was his answer. Finally, the Ugandan pastor had peace. Elijah's smile returned and he began eating and enjoying the blessings of the plentiful nation he'd come to visit. "I knew then, God had given me a message to speak to the people of America: *God has blessed you with more than what you need, that you may be a blessing to the rest of the world.*"

When God Speaks

"Up to this day . . . truly, whenever I land in America, I cry. That is the truth, I cry! I remember how my people suffer. And whenever I return to Uganda, I cry. You look at the plane landing. You look at the people—someone needs only five dollars to change his life. A Hands of Love child needs fifty dollars a month and it will change everything. Everything *will change*."

Satisfied with God's answer and emboldened to speak it throughout the land of "more than enough," Elijah carries this message forth today. He tells his story of faith and suffering, of how he lived without, to those who live with much. He speaks to the generous Jays and the Will Hankins's and the CEOs and the privileged children of America.

They hear God's message and consider His invitation extend their hand and "be the blessing."

Look Beyond Yourself

My Ugandan friends are grateful to be on the receiving end of America's blessings. But they don't sit around twiddling their thumbs, waiting for handouts. Rather, they look at what *they* can do and what *they* can give. They have giant faith that believes "even though I have next to nothing, I can be God's hands of love." And they graciously *share* the incredible privilege of partnering with God in His work as more servants arrive from Charleston, South Carolina and other corners of the world.

One of the women from Elijah's church fosters seven orphans. She lives three miles from the church. On Wednesdays and Sundays, the woman walks six miles in dollar-store flip-flops that are nearly worn through. This woman has taken to heart Elijah's challenge to be stronger. "A strong man lives for himself. A stronger man lives for others," he says. "God is looking for stronger men, people who live for others."

One day, a man who noticed the woman's route visited Hands of Love and asked Elijah about the woman. He donated twenty-five dollars for her to buy a decent pair of walking shoes. This man lives for others. He is a stronger man.

But the story doesn't end there.

Because God is also looking for strong women. The flip-flop wearing widow saved the shoe money for three months. Despite her own needs, she looked beyond herself and asked, "Is there a bigger purpose for this money than to buy myself shoes?" She believed God had another way, a bigger way, for her to spend the twenty-five dollar gift. So, she waited.

Three months later, Elijah told his congregation that several Hands of Love children were sleeping outside due to lack of space. "I told the church that we needed to quickly come up with a solution. This widow, she lifted up her hand before I finished speaking and said, 'That is what I was waiting for from God. To use my only money on a bigger purpose than myself.'" Elijah rejoiced as the widow's twenty-five dollars was multiplied: eleven of the paid staff members donated fifty percent of their money as well. Within a few days, construction began on a small sleeping dormitory.

When God Speaks

The self-sacrifice and heroic faith of my poor brothers and sisters in Uganda makes me wonder: Does living in our blessed nation of plenty, one that is plagued by excess and materialism, diminish our faith? Is it a stumbling block for those who have much? The Bible says it's easier for a camel to pass through the eye of a needle than for a rich man to enter the kingdom of God[48]. It also says blessed are the poor in spirit for they shall inherit the kingdom of God. And I've seen Uganda's suffering and marveled at how God uses poverty and difficulties to strengthen faith.

"The moment you continue focusing on yourself, you lose focus on God. So you lose God and develop a relationship with *a god*. That is trouble," Elijah says. "This god of materialism will never drink enough, never drive enough, never eat enough, never have enough—it will always open its mouth to put in more, more, more. The only way we can tell this god to leave is by looking beyond ourselves. The moment you do that, this god called materialism will receive a special command to leave. And then this god will leave, just as Jesus commanded Satan to go."

I believe what Elijah says because I have seen it—gigantic faith growing out of looking beyond myself. As I attempt to "be the blessing," I donate my time and limited abilities to broadcast God's Hands of Love story. In return, I have the unparalleled honor of serving beside those who have suffered and endured horrific things unlike anything I've experienced. Their

---

[48] Matthew 10:25;19:24 and Luke 18:25

suffering has seasoned their faith and deepened their belief in God far beyond mine. These kings and queens of faith serve *me* coffee, cold bottles of water, and bananas. They answer my endless questions, share their stories and their hearts, and pray for God to bless *my family (*we who dwell in the land of plenty.) I am the privileged partner to those saints of Uganda. Truly, it is my privilege and they are doing me the favor.

In God's upside-down economy, the flip-flop wearing widow is rich and the Rolex-wearing executive is poor, because blessed are the ones who wear worn shoes for theirs is the kingdom of heaven.

And I hunger for their outrageous faith.

To get it, must I exorcise the demon of materialism and sell all my possessions like the rich man Jesus talked about? God told Elijah that Americans have been blessed to be a blessing. I guess each of us must figure out how God is calling us to "be the blessing."

Like Anna Latshaw did …

*****

When Hands of Love USA founder Anna Latshaw met Elijah, she was a mom of four and her youngest was four weeks old. As she weighed the sacrifices of becoming involved, "it should have been a much harder decision," she says. Anna's desire to look beyond herself—including her own weaknesses and limitations—demonstrated big faith in action.

When God Speaks

"God took away my rational thinking. I didn't question whether I should help, even though I lacked the business background and organizational skills. God was in this. So I just did what I could and trusted God to do the rest."

Watching God work while writing Elijah's story has grown my faith. Watching God gather 188 orphans . . . stand with Elijah in front of that lion . . . lay next to him, face down in the dirty pools of blood . . . and seeing God deliver my friend over and over again. That vicarious journey has afforded me a great gift. A gift that keeps on giving, that will never tarnish, fade, or be destroyed by moths[49].

With deeper faith, I reach out to the God of the Impossible. I take His hand and, with the other, I extend it to others, and become the blessing. May the ripple effects be astounding. Not for my fame, Lord. But for Yours alone.

---

[49] "Do not store up for yourselves treasures on earth, where moth and rust destroy, and where thieves break in and steal. But store up for yourselves treasures in heaven, where neither moth nor rust destroys, and where thieves do not break in or steal" (Matthew 6:19-20).

When God Speaks

Meet Pastor Elijah Sebuchu

Our founder, Pastor Elijah Sebuchu, grew up in extreme poverty in rural Uganda. As one of 38 children in a polygamous family, he slept on the ground without a blanket for most of his childhood and almost died from insect infestations as a result at the age of eight. He received his first pair of shoes at age 15 and at 18, for the first time in his life, felt the satisfaction of a full stomach.

Pastor Elijah was privileged to have been raised by his godly mother Esther. She daily spoke powerful authoritative words of prophecy in his life, telling him that he was born to lead and that he would not die like so many others. She also taught her son important life lessons and biblical principles that began to shape and guide Elijah.

Although his childhood was miserable in many respects, Pastor Elijah received an education, unlike most of the poor in his country. He took advantage of this opportunity, completed undergraduate degrees and earned a seminary degree from a local university. It wasn't until after he graduated, however, that Pastor Elijah came to know Jesus Christ as his personal Lord and Savior. He began pursuing God's calling on his life. He became an evangelist, opened his own church in the capital city, Kampala International Christian Centre (KICC), and started planting churches throughout the countryside of Uganda.

When God Speaks

As God was growing Pastor Elijah's church ministry, God began opening Elijah's eyes and heart to the droves of wandering orphans in his country. He realized that there were not enough resources in Uganda to meet the needs of the orphans and began sending pleas over the internet for international help. Through a miraculous sequence of events, God provided connections and a network of people who helped Elijah build Hands of Love Orphanages and School.

Elijah and his wife, Ruth, live and serve in Kampala, Uganda and have five biological children. Under their umbrella organization, Global Discipleship Ministries (GDM) and together with the many laborers in Uganda, Elijah and Ruth now serve over 70 churches directly and over 300 Partner Churches indirectly. GDM's ministries include:

- Two Hands of Love Orphanages and Schools with over 2,600 orphans and abandoned children
- Maama Eseza Babies Home which rescues and nurtures children under the age of three
- Spiritual and church leadership training to 271 Ugandan pastors and their constituents
- 24-7 radio ministry that reaches 30 million Ugandans
- Weekly discipleship groups
- Annual conferences including the Pastors & Leaders Conference, Youth Ablaze, and Women's Empowerment

Even though thousands of lives are being transformed daily through GDM, the vision that God has given to Pastor Elijah Sebuchu and to Hands of

Love Foundation is to save thousands more. With God's guidance and your partnership, we will continue in our mission to transform a nation, one soul at a time.

When God Speaks

History of Hands of Love Foundation

2004

Hands of Love begins with seven mud huts and

188 children in rural Namadhi, Uganda.

When God Speaks

2005

The first western missionary visits the Hands of Love orphanage and launches our child sponsorship program by obtaining sponsors for six children.

When God Speaks

2006

Hands of Love UK is founded for support and to expand the sponsorship program.

2006

The first Hands of Love Primary School is opened in the Namadhi orphanage.

2008

Hands of Love USA is founded for support and to increase sponsorship.

2009

The second Hands of Love orphanage and school is built in Kabaga-Kampala. Now the older children have access to high school education, which is unavailable in Namadhi.

2010

The number of children being cared for in both orphanages reaches 1,000. More dormitory and classrooms are built.

When God Speaks

2012

Water wells are built at the Kabaga-Kampala and Namadhi orphanages. The children's hygiene and wellness improve dramatically.

2012

Electricity is turned on in the Kabaga-Kampala orphanage. Most of the children have never had access to electricity and the safety it can provide.

2013

Namadhi is outfitted with solar power.

For the first time, these children have access to electrical power.

2013

Convoy of Hope, a faith-based organization that provides disaster relief across the world, agrees to partner with us to help feed our children.

2015

The number of children in our care reaches 1600.
Additional classrooms and dormitories are built.

2016

The Hands of Love Medical Centre opens. The Center provides healthcare services to women and children and to the children and staff of Hands of Love.

2016

The Maama Eseza Babies' Home opens to rescue and nurture orphaned and abandoned babies, newborn to age three.

2016

The Hands of Love Kabaga-Kampala Primary School is ranked 3rd best out of 48,000 Ugandan schools and has the top two ranking Math students in the country.

2016

The number of children in our care reaches 2,000.

2017

The first class of 25 students graduate from Hands of Love with either high school degrees or vocational school degrees. Less than 2% of Uganda's population currently completes high school

When God Speaks

2019

God is Able Building was completed, seen here receiving its final coat of paint, and recently retrofitted with running water and toilets. A beautiful place for our children to learn and grow.

2019

Staff Housing construction began and is progressing nicely. Two floors of this four-story project have been funded and will accommodate 24 staff members and their families once completed in 2020-21.

Made in the USA
Columbia, SC
12 November 2020